Java Development: Master Object-Oriented Programming

A Complete Guide to Java's Core Features and Techniques

BOOZMAN RICHARD

BOOKER BLUNT

Table of Content

TABLE OF CONTENTS

INTRODUCTION

The Java development landscape has evolved dramatically over the past decade, with JavaScript frameworks playing a pivotal role in shaping how developers build interactive, dynamic, and scalable applications. In this rapidly changing ecosystem, staying up to date with the latest frameworks and technologies is crucial to building high-performance web applications that meet user expectations for speed, reliability, and seamless experiences across devices.

This book, *Java Development: Master Oriented Programming* , is designed to be your comprehensive guide to mastering the most popular JavaScript frameworks used in modern web development. Whether you are just starting your journey into web development or you're a seasoned developer looking to deepen your knowledge, this book covers everything you need to know about **React**, **Angular**, and **Vue.js**. Each chapter is crafted to provide you with a clear understanding of the core concepts, best practices, and real-world examples, helping you build scalable, maintainable, and performant applications.

Why This Book Is Essential

The demand for rich, interactive web applications has never been higher. With the rise of Single Page Applications (SPAs), Progressive Web Apps (PWAs), and mobile-first design, developers must not only understand the principles of front-end development but also leverage modern JavaScript frameworks to enhance the user experience and meet the growing demands of today's digital world.

In this book, you will:

- Gain a deep understanding of **React**, **Angular**, and **Vue.js**, each of which has its unique strengths and weaknesses.
- Learn how to implement best practices for building fast, efficient, and secure web applications.
- Dive into advanced topics such as **state management**, **routing**, **service workers**, and **performance optimization**.
- Explore real-world examples of building web apps from scratch, including integrating APIs, securing user data, and optimizing performance.

- Get hands-on experience with building **Progressive Web Apps (PWAs)**, **Single Page Applications (SPAs)**, and mobile-first web solutions.

Whether you're looking to improve your skills in building scalable front-end applications or need to stay updated with the latest trends and technologies in web development, this book will serve as your essential companion.

What You Will Learn

In the first part of the book, we'll explore the foundational concepts of JavaScript frameworks. You'll get acquainted with the core principles behind **React**, **Angular**, and **Vue.js**, including their strengths, weaknesses, and appropriate use cases. We'll dive into the fundamentals of each framework, helping you choose the right tool for your next project.

Next, we will cover how to build real-world applications with these frameworks. You'll learn how to develop powerful web apps by creating dynamic user interfaces, managing state effectively, and implementing modern features like **routing**, **authentication**, and **data binding**. You'll also get hands-on experience building **single-page**

applications (SPAs) and integrating APIs to enhance the functionality of your app.

As we move deeper into advanced topics, the book will guide you through **state management** using libraries like **Redux** for React, **NgRx** for Angular, and **Vuex** for Vue.js. We'll also focus on performance optimization techniques such as **code splitting**, **lazy loading**, **caching**, and **progressive web apps (PWAs)** to ensure that your web apps perform at their best across all devices and network conditions.

Security is also a major concern when developing web applications. In this book, we'll explore how to protect your app from common vulnerabilities like **Cross-Site Scripting (XSS)**, **Cross-Site Request Forgery (CSRF)**, and **SQL Injection**. You'll learn how to implement secure authentication systems using **JWT** (JSON Web Tokens) and other modern techniques to safeguard your app's data and user privacy.

The final section of the book covers best practices and strategies for maintaining and evolving your web apps. We'll focus on **test-driven development (TDD)**, **unit testing**, and **end-to-end testing** with tools like **Jest, Karma,** and **Protractor**. We'll also discuss how to stay up to date with the latest trends and frameworks in the JavaScript ecosystem, ensuring your skills remain relevant in the ever-changing world of web development.

Who This Book Is For

This book is intended for developers of all experience levels who want to master modern JavaScript frameworks. Whether you are:

- A **beginner** looking to get started with React, Angular, or Vue.js, and want to learn the fundamentals of web development with modern frameworks.
- An **intermediate developer** who wants to deepen your understanding of state management, routing, testing, and performance optimization.
- An **experienced developer** seeking to stay updated on the latest tools, best practices, and trends in JavaScript frameworks, and how to build scalable, secure, and high-performance web applications.

Why React, Angular, and Vue.js?

The three frameworks covered in this book—**React**, **Angular**, and **Vue.js**—are the most widely used and popular choices for building web applications today. Each framework has unique features, and understanding their strengths and use cases will help you choose the right one for your project.

- **React**: Known for its simplicity and flexibility, React is a **JavaScript library** for building user interfaces. Its component-based architecture and virtual DOM make it highly efficient for rendering dynamic UIs, and it is widely adopted for creating modern, fast web applications.

- **Angular**: Angular is a **full-fledged framework** that provides everything you need for building large-scale web applications. With built-in tools like **dependency injection**, **routing**, and **forms management**, Angular is perfect for building complex, enterprise-level apps.

- **Vue.js**: Vue is a **progressive framework** that is both easy to learn and flexible enough to scale for large applications. It combines the best features of both React and Angular, offering an approachable learning curve with powerful tools for building dynamic, modern web apps.

By the end of this book, you'll have a solid understanding of these frameworks and the ability to build robust, production-ready web apps with them.

Conclusion

The world of JavaScript frameworks is constantly evolving, and staying up-to-date with the latest tools and techniques is essential for becoming a proficient web developer. *Java Development: Master Oriented Programming* offers a detailed, hands-on guide to building modern web applications that are fast, scalable, and secure. By mastering these frameworks, you'll be equipped to tackle any web development challenge and stay at the forefront of the ever-changing landscape of web technologies.

Whether you're building a personal project or working on an enterprise-level application, the skills and knowledge you gain from this book will serve as a solid foundation for your future web development career. Let's dive in and explore the power of **React**, **Angular**, and **Vue.js**, and start building modern web apps that users love!

CHAPTER 1

INTRODUCTION TO JAVA AND OBJECT-ORIENTED PROGRAMMING (OOP)

Overview of Java and Its Importance in Modern Development

Java is one of the most widely used programming languages in the world. Originally developed by Sun Microsystems in 1995 and now maintained by Oracle, Java has become a cornerstone of modern software development. It is known for its platform independence, thanks to the "Write Once, Run Anywhere" (WORA) principle, which means that Java code can run on any device with a Java Virtual Machine (JVM). This versatility has made Java the preferred choice for large-scale applications, mobile app development (Android), web applications, and even embedded systems.

Java's strong emphasis on reliability, maintainability, and scalability has made it the go-to language for building enterprise-level applications. In fact, Java is at the heart of many financial systems, banking applications, and cloud platforms. Java's ability to handle complex, large-scale applications with ease has made it indispensable in modern software development.

What is Object-Oriented Programming (OOP)?

Object-Oriented Programming (OOP) is a programming paradigm based on the concept of "objects." An object is a self-contained entity that includes both data (attributes) and methods (functions) that operate on the data. OOP focuses on organizing software design around these objects rather than functions or logic. This approach allows developers to build more modular, reusable, and maintainable code.

In OOP, the core focus is on how objects interact with one another, and how they encapsulate data and behavior. OOP is based on four key principles: **Encapsulation**, **Inheritance**, **Polymorphism**, and **Abstraction**. These principles serve as the foundation for designing software that is both flexible and easy to maintain.

Key Principles of OOP

1. **Encapsulation**: Encapsulation is the process of bundling the data (attributes) and the methods (functions) that operate on the data within a single unit, called a class. This principle helps in hiding the internal workings of an object and only exposing the necessary parts through well-defined interfaces, like getters and setters. The main goal is to protect the object's data from unauthorized access or modification and to ensure that it is used only in valid ways.

14

- o **Real-World Example**: Think of a **bank account**. The account balance is an internal piece of data that should not be accessed directly by outsiders. Instead, the bank provides methods like `deposit()` and `withdraw()` to interact with the balance safely.

2. **Inheritance**: Inheritance allows a class to inherit the properties and behaviors (methods) of another class. This helps in code reuse and creates a hierarchical relationship between classes. The child class can extend the functionality of the parent class or override its methods to specialize its behavior.

    - o **Real-World Example**: Consider a **Vehicle** class with common properties like `speed` and `fuel`. A **Car** class can inherit from the **Vehicle** class, and add its own specific properties, like `airConditioning` or `sunroof`. A **Truck** class can also inherit from **Vehicle** but may add features like `cargoCapacity`.

3. **Polymorphism**: Polymorphism allows an object to take on many forms. In Java, this is typically achieved through method overriding (runtime polymorphism) or method overloading (compile-time polymorphism). Polymorphism allows objects of different classes to be treated as objects of a common superclass, simplifying code and improving flexibility.

○ **Real-World Example**: A **Shape** class with a method `draw()` can have multiple subclasses such as **Circle**, **Rectangle**, and **Triangle**, each overriding the `draw()` method to implement its specific version of drawing the shape. Even though you refer to them as a **Shape**, each class has its own behavior when `draw()` is called.

4. **Abstraction**: Abstraction involves hiding the complex implementation details of a system and exposing only the essential features. This is typically done through abstract classes or interfaces. Abstraction helps in reducing complexity by focusing only on the necessary aspects of an object's behavior, leaving out the irrelevant details.

○ **Real-World Example**: Consider a **Smartphone**. The abstraction hides the internal complexities of how the phone operates (e.g., the operating system, hardware, and other low-level components) and provides the user with a simple interface, such as tapping icons to open apps or making a call.

Java's Role in OOP and Why It's Widely Used in Enterprise Applications

Java is inherently designed to support Object-Oriented Programming. From the ground up, Java encourages developers to create software in an object-oriented way. Every Java application is based around the concept of objects, with classes forming the blueprint for those objects.

Java's emphasis on OOP brings several advantages, especially in enterprise applications:

- **Maintainability**: Object-Oriented systems are easier to maintain because they are organized into well-defined, self-contained objects. Changes to one object do not require changes to others unless they are tightly coupled, making the system more flexible.
- **Reusability**: Java allows developers to reuse code via inheritance and interfaces. By creating libraries of reusable objects or methods, organizations can save time and resources in future projects.
- **Scalability**: Java's object-oriented nature allows it to scale well. It's possible to extend the functionality of existing systems without rewriting them, making Java ideal for growing enterprise applications.
- **Security**: Java's encapsulation feature ensures that data is protected from unauthorized access, which is crucial in secure enterprise applications.

Enterprise applications often require large teams to develop, maintain, and scale over time. Java's object-oriented features, combined with its robust ecosystem (Java EE, Spring, Hibernate), make it an ideal choice for such complex systems. Additionally,

Java's rich set of libraries and frameworks further enhances its usability in various business domains.

Real-World Examples Where Java's OOP Features Are Used

1. **Banking Systems**: Banks use Java's OOP features to build secure, scalable applications for managing customer accounts, transactions, and other financial services. For example, the **Account** class might encapsulate account details, while the **Transaction** class might model individual transactions, and **Bank** class might represent the overall banking system.

2. **E-Commerce Platforms**: Java is used to build e-commerce platforms where polymorphism and inheritance come into play. The **Product** class could have subclasses like **Book, Clothing**, and **Electronics**, each implementing its specific behavior for handling pricing, discounts, and availability.

3. **Telecommunication Systems**: Telecom companies use Java to manage millions of users and devices, employing OOP to model complex systems. For instance, the **Device** class could serve as a base class, while subclasses like **MobilePhone** and **Tablet** define more specific behaviors and attributes.

4. **Healthcare Applications**: In healthcare, Java is often used to build systems for managing patient records, appointments, and medical histories. Java's object-

oriented features help to model complex relationships between patients, doctors, and appointments, ensuring that the data is organized, secure, and easy to maintain.

This chapter introduces the foundational principles of OOP and explains how Java implements them. By providing real-world examples, the chapter sets the stage for a deeper exploration of Java's features and their applications in modern software development.

CHAPTER 2

SETTING UP JAVA DEVELOPMENT ENVIRONMENT

Installing Java Development Kit (JDK) and Integrated Development Environment (IDE)

Before you can start writing and running Java programs, you need to install two essential components:

1. **Java Development Kit (JDK)**: The JDK is a software development kit used to develop Java applications. It includes the Java Runtime Environment (JRE), which provides libraries and components for running Java programs, as well as tools like the Java compiler (javac) to compile Java code, and the Java debugger (jdb) to troubleshoot code.

   Installation Steps:

   o **Step 1**: Download the latest JDK version from the official Oracle website or from open-source distributions like AdoptOpenJDK.

   o **Step 2**: Run the installer for your operating system (Windows, macOS, or Linux). Follow the installation instructions, ensuring that you select the option to set the JDK as the system path during installation.

- o **Step 3**: Verify the installation by opening your terminal or command prompt and typing:

```
nginx
```

```
java -version
```

This should display the version of Java that is installed.

2. **Setting Up the IDE**: The next step is to install an Integrated Development Environment (IDE). An IDE provides a graphical interface for writing, compiling, and debugging code, making development easier. Popular Java IDEs include **Eclipse**, **IntelliJ IDEA**, and **NetBeans**.

Introduction to Popular IDEs (Eclipse, IntelliJ IDEA, NetBeans)

1. **Eclipse**:
   - o **Overview**: Eclipse is an open-source IDE widely used for Java development. It has a vast ecosystem of plugins that allow you to add features for web development, mobile development, and more.

21

- o **Features**:
    - Integrated debugging tools.
    - Built-in version control support (e.g., Git).
    - Powerful refactoring tools.
    - Extensive community support and plugins.

Installation:

- o Visit the Eclipse Downloads Page and download the appropriate version for your operating system.
- o After installation, open Eclipse, set a workspace directory where all your projects will be saved, and you're ready to start coding!

2. **IntelliJ IDEA**:
    - o **Overview**: IntelliJ IDEA is a popular IDE known for its ease of use, powerful features, and excellent support for Java. It offers both a free Community edition and a paid Ultimate edition.
    - o **Features**:
        - Smart code completion and refactoring tools.
        - Excellent support for frameworks like Spring and Hibernate.
        - Powerful debugging and testing tools.

- Seamless integration with version control systems like Git and SVN.

Installation:

- ○ Download IntelliJ IDEA from the JetBrains website.
- ○ Choose the Community Edition (free) or the Ultimate Edition (paid) based on your needs.
- ○ After installation, you can configure the IDE to use your JDK and start writing Java code.

3. **NetBeans**:

- ○ **Overview**: NetBeans is another open-source IDE that is easy to use, especially for beginners. It supports Java, HTML5, JavaScript, PHP, and many other languages.
- ○ **Features**:
  - Simple user interface, making it great for beginners.
  - Support for JavaFX and web development.
  - Integrated tools for debugging and profiling.
  - Good integration with databases and web servers.

Installation:

- o Download NetBeans from the Apache NetBeans website.
- o Install the IDE and open it. You will need to configure your JDK and start writing Java programs right away.

How to Set Up and Configure Your Development Environment

Once you've chosen and installed your IDE, it's time to configure the development environment for Java.

1. **Setting up Java in Eclipse**:
   - o After installing Eclipse, open the IDE and go to the **Window** menu.
   - o Select **Preferences**, then go to **Java > Installed JREs**.
   - o Click on **Add External JRE** to select your installed JDK folder (typically located in `C:\Program Files\Java\jdk-x.x.x` on Windows).
   - o Set the JDK as the default and click **OK**.
2. **Setting up Java in IntelliJ IDEA**:
   - o Open IntelliJ IDEA and create a new Java project.
   - o In the "New Project" window, select **Java** from the project type.

o   IntelliJ IDEA will prompt you to select a JDK. Choose the installed JDK from the list or point to the directory where your JDK is located.

o   Once the project is created, you can start writing Java code.

3. **Setting up Java in NetBeans**:

o   Launch NetBeans and navigate to **Tools** > **Java Platforms**.

o   Click **Add Platform** and select your installed JDK.

o   Once the JDK is configured, NetBeans will automatically use it when you create new projects.

First "Hello World" Program and Its Breakdown

Now that your environment is set up, let's write and run your first Java program: **"Hello, World!"**

Code Example:

```java

public class HelloWorld {
    public static void main(String[] args) {
        System.out.println("Hello, World!");
    }
```

25

```
}
```

Code Breakdown:

- **public class HelloWorld**: This line declares a class named `HelloWorld`. In Java, every program must be contained within a class. The keyword `public` means that the class is accessible from anywhere.

- **public static void main(String[] args)**: This is the entry point of every Java program. The `main` method is where the program starts execution. `String[] args` is used to receive command-line arguments, though it is not used in this example.

- **System.out.println("Hello, World!");**: This line of code prints the string `"Hello, World!"` to the console. `System.out` refers to the standard output stream (the console), and `println` is a method used to print a line of text.

Running the Program:

- **In Eclipse**: Right-click on the file and select **Run As > Java Application**.

- **In IntelliJ IDEA**: Click the green "Run" button located at the top-right corner of the IDE.

- **In NetBeans**: Right-click on the project and select **Run**.

Upon running the program, you should see the output:

```
Hello, World!
```

This simple program is the first step in getting familiar with Java syntax and setting up your development environment. As you progress, you'll learn more advanced concepts, but the **Hello World** program remains a fundamental exercise for any developer.

With your Java environment fully configured and your first program running, you're ready to dive deeper into Java programming. In the next chapters, we will explore Java syntax in more detail, along with the core principles of Object-Oriented Programming that will serve as the foundation for more complex Java development.

CHAPTER 3

UNDERSTANDING JAVA SYNTAX

Java syntax is the set of rules that define the structure of valid Java programs. Understanding Java syntax is crucial for writing well-structured, efficient, and readable code. In this chapter, we will explore the basic structure of a Java program, as well as data types, variables, constants, operators, expressions, and control flow mechanisms such as conditional statements and loops.

Basic Structure of a Java Program

A typical Java program consists of several key components. Let's break down the basic structure:

1. **Class Declaration**: Every Java program must have at least one class. The class serves as the blueprint for creating objects in Java.

```java

public class MyClass {
}
```

2. **Main Method**: The main method is the entry point of the program. When you run a Java application, the JVM starts by executing the code inside the `main` method.

```java
public static void main(String[] args) {
}
```

3. **Statements and Blocks**: Code inside the class is written as statements. Statements are the actions that the program performs. A group of statements can be enclosed in curly braces { } to form a block.

```java
public class MyClass {
    public static void main(String[] args)
{
        System.out.println("Hello,
Java!"); // A statement
    }
}
```

In the above example:

- **public class MyClass** declares a class named MyClass.

- `public static void main(String[] args)` is the main method where the execution starts.
- `System.out.println("Hello, Java!");` is a statement that prints the string to the console.

Data Types, Variables, and Constants

1. **Data Types**: Java is a statically typed language, meaning you must specify the data type of a variable before using it. There are two types of data types in Java:
   - **Primitive Data Types**: These are built-in data types that represent simple values.
     - `int`: Integer numbers (e.g., 5, 100, -42).
     - `double`: Floating-point numbers for decimal values (e.g., 3.14, -7.5).
     - `char`: Single characters (e.g., 'a', '1').
     - `boolean`: True or false values (e.g., `true`, `false`).
     - `byte`, `short`, `long`: Used for different sizes of integers.
     - `float`: Single-precision floating-point numbers.
   - **Reference Data Types**: These refer to objects, arrays, or instances of classes. They include classes, interfaces, and arrays.

2. **Variables**: A variable is a named storage location in memory where data is stored. To declare a variable, you must specify its data type followed by its name:

```java
int age = 30;   // A variable of type int
double price = 19.99;   // A variable of type double
```

3. **Constants**: Constants are variables whose values cannot be changed once they are assigned. In Java, constants are declared using the `final` keyword:

```java
final double PI = 3.14159;   // A constant for the value of pi
```

Operators and Expressions

1. **Operators**: Operators are special symbols used to perform operations on variables and values. In Java, operators are categorized into the following types:

   o **Arithmetic Operators**: Used for mathematical operations.

   ```java
   ```

```
int sum = 5 + 3;   // Addition
int diff = 5 - 3;   // Subtraction
int product = 5 * 3;      //
Multiplication
int quotient = 5 / 3;   // Division
int remainder = 5 % 3;   // Modulus
(remainder)
```

- o **Relational Operators**: Used to compare two values.

```
java
```

```
boolean isEqual = 5 == 3;   // Equals
to
boolean isGreaterThan = 5 > 3;   //
Greater than
boolean isLessThan = 5 < 3;   // Less
than
```

- o **Logical Operators**: Used to combine multiple boolean expressions.

```
java
```

```
boolean result = true && false;   //
AND operator
boolean result2 = true || false;   //
OR operator
```

```
boolean  result3  =  !true;    //  NOT
operator
```

- o **Assignment Operators**: Used to assign values to variables.

```java

int x = 5;  // Assigns 5 to x
x += 3;   // x = x + 3
x *= 2;   // x = x * 2
```

2. **Expressions**: An expression is a combination of variables, constants, and operators that the Java interpreter evaluates to produce a value. For example:

```java

int result = (5 + 3) * 2;   // Expression
that evaluates to 16
```

In the above example, 5 + 3 is evaluated first, then the result is multiplied by 2.

Conditional Statements (if, switch) and Loops (for, while, do-while)

1. **Conditional Statements**: Conditional statements allow you to execute different blocks of code based on specific

conditions. In Java, the most commonly used conditional statements are if, else if, and switch.

- o **if Statement**: Used to execute a block of code if a condition is true.

java

```
int x = 10;
if (x > 5) {
    System.out.println("x is greater
than 5");
}
```

- o **else if and else**: Used for multiple conditions.

java

```
int x = 10;
if (x > 10) {
    System.out.println("x is greater
than 10");
} else if (x == 10) {
    System.out.println("x  is  equal
to 10");
} else {
    System.out.println("x   is   less
than 10");
}
```

- o **switch Statement**: Used to handle multiple conditions based on a variable's value.

```java

int day = 2;
switch (day) {
    case 1:

System.out.println("Monday");
        break;
    case 2:

System.out.println("Tuesday");
        break;
    default:
        System.out.println("Invalid
day");
}
```

2. **Loops**: Loops allow you to execute a block of code repeatedly under certain conditions.
   - o **for Loop**: Ideal for situations where the number of iterations is known beforehand.

```java

for (int i = 0; i < 5; i++) {
    System.out.println(i);
```

```
}
// Output: 0, 1, 2, 3, 4
```

o **while Loop**: Executes the block of code as long as the specified condition is true.

```java
int i = 0;
while (i < 5) {
    System.out.println(i);
    i++;
}
// Output: 0, 1, 2, 3, 4
```

o **do-while Loop**: Similar to the `while` loop, but the block of code is executed at least once before checking the condition.

```java
int i = 0;
do {
    System.out.println(i);
    i++;
} while (i < 5);
// Output: 0, 1, 2, 3, 4
```

Summary

In this chapter, we've covered the fundamental building blocks of Java syntax:

- **Basic Program Structure**: Every Java program must have a class and a main method where execution begins.
- **Data Types, Variables, and Constants**: We explored primitive and reference data types, how to declare variables, and how to use constants with the `final` keyword.
- **Operators and Expressions**: We examined arithmetic, relational, logical, and assignment operators, along with expressions used to compute and manipulate values.
- **Conditional Statements and Loops**: We looked at `if`, `else if`, `else`, `switch`, and loop structures (`for`, `while`, and `do-while`) for controlling the flow of the program based on conditions.

With these building blocks in place, you're now ready to write more complex Java programs. In the next chapters, we will dive deeper into Java's Object-Oriented features and start applying these concepts to real-world projects.

CHAPTER 4

BASIC OBJECT-ORIENTED CONCEPTS

Object-Oriented Programming (OOP) is a programming paradigm that organizes software design around objects, rather than functions and logic. In Java, understanding basic object-oriented concepts is essential as they form the foundation for building more complex systems. This chapter will cover the key concepts of classes and objects, constructors, instance variables vs. class variables, and a real-world analogy to help you visualize these concepts.

Creating and Using Classes and Objects

1. **Classes**: A **class** in Java is a blueprint or template for creating objects. It defines the properties (fields) and behaviors (methods) that the objects created from the class will have. In essence, a class describes how an object will look and how it will behave.

   Syntax for defining a class:

   ```java
   ```

```java
public class Car {
    // Fields or attributes
    String make;
    String model;
    int year;

    // Method or behavior
    public void startEngine() {
        System.out.println("The engine is
now running.");
    }
}
```

In this example, `Car` is the class, and it has three fields (`make`, `model`, and `year`), and one method (`startEngine()`) that describes the behavior of the object.

2. **Objects**: An **object** is an instance of a class. Once a class is defined, you can create objects from that class using the `new` keyword. Each object holds its own data, independent of other objects.

   Creating an object:

   ```
   java
   ```

   ```java
   public class Main {
   ```

39

```
    public static void main(String[] args)
{
        // Creating an object of the Car
class
        Car myCar = new Car();
        myCar.make = "Toyota";
        myCar.model = "Corolla";
        myCar.year = 2020;
        myCar.startEngine();
    }
}
```

Here, `myCar` is an object of the `Car` class. We use the `new` keyword to create an instance of the `Car` class, and then set its properties using dot notation (`myCar.make` = `"Toyota"`).

Constructors and Their Role in Java

A **constructor** in Java is a special type of method that is used to initialize objects when they are created. Constructors have the same name as the class and are called automatically when you create an object.

1. **Default Constructor**: If you do not explicitly define a constructor, Java provides a default constructor with no

arguments that initializes the object with default values (e.g., `null` for object types, 0 for integers).

Example of a default constructor:

java

```
public class Car {
    String make;
    String model;
    int year;

    // Default constructor
    public Car() {
        make = "Unknown";
        model = "Unknown";
        year = 0;
    }
}
```

2. **Parameterized Constructor**: You can define your own constructor to initialize an object with specific values when it is created. This is known as a parameterized constructor.

Example of a parameterized constructor:

java

```
public class Car {
    String make;
    String model;
    int year;

    // Parameterized constructor
    public Car(String make, String model,
int year) {
        this.make = make;
        this.model = model;
        this.year = year;
    }
}
```

With this constructor, you can pass specific values when creating a new object:

java

```
public class Main {
    public static void main(String[] args)
{
        // Creating an object of the Car
class using the parameterized constructor
        Car myCar = new Car("Toyota",
"Corolla", 2020);
        System.out.println(myCar.make + "
" + myCar.model + " " + myCar.year);
    }
}
```

Output:

```yaml
Toyota Corolla 2020
```

In the parameterized constructor, the `this` keyword refers to the current object and helps distinguish between the instance variables (e.g., `make`, `model`, `year`) and the method parameters (e.g., `make`, `model`, `year`).

Instance Variables vs. Class Variables

1. **Instance Variables**: Instance variables are non-static fields that are unique to each object created from the class. Each object has its own of the instance variables. They represent the properties of individual objects.

   Example:

   ```java
   public class Car {
       // Instance variables
       String make;
       String model;
       int year;
   }
   ```

43

Every object of the `Car` class will have its own `make`, `model`, and `year` values.

2. **Class Variables**: Class variables, also known as **static variables**, are shared among all instances (objects) of a class. They are declared using the `static` keyword. Unlike instance variables, class variables have only one , regardless of how many objects are created.

Example:

```java
public class Car {
    // Class variable (static)
    static int numberOfCars = 0;

    String make;
    String model;
    int year;

    public Car(String make, String model,
int year) {
        this.make = make;
        this.model = model;
        this.year = year;
        numberOfCars++;   // Increment the
number of cars created
    }
```

```
}
```

Here, `numberOfCars` is a static variable that keeps track of how many `Car` objects have been created. No matter how many `Car` objects are instantiated, all objects share this one variable.

java

```
public class Main {
    public static void main(String[] args)
{
        Car  car1  =  new  Car("Toyota",
"Camry", 2020);
        Car  car2  =  new  Car("Honda",
"Civic", 2021);
        System.out.println("Total  cars:  "
+ Car.numberOfCars);  // Output will be 2
    }
}
```

Real-World Analogy for Classes and Objects

To make the concept of classes and objects more understandable, let's consider a real-world analogy:

1. **Class**: A class is like a **blueprint** or **template**. It defines the characteristics and behaviors of a type of object but

does not represent a specific object itself. For instance, a **Car blueprint** defines what a car can have (attributes like make, model, and year) and what a car can do (behaviors like starting the engine).

2. **Object**: An object is an **instance** of the class, like a **specific car** built from the car blueprint. Each object can have different values for its attributes, like a red Toyota Corolla or a blue Honda Accord. These cars are unique objects, but they all follow the same blueprint defined by the `Car` class.

Real-world analogy:

- o **Class**: Car (general blueprint)
- o **Object**: myCar (a specific instance of the Car class)

Summary

In this chapter, we've introduced the core concepts of object-oriented programming in Java:

- **Classes and Objects**: A class is a template for creating objects, while an object is an instance of that class.
- **Constructors**: Special methods used to initialize objects. The default constructor initializes objects with default

46

values, while parameterized constructors allow you to set specific values during object creation.

- **Instance Variables vs. Class Variables**: Instance variables are unique to each object, while class variables are shared across all instances of the class.
- **Real-World Analogy**: Classes are blueprints for creating objects, which are specific instances of those blueprints.

Understanding these fundamental concepts will allow you to start building complex systems using Java. In the next chapters, we will dive deeper into the advanced features of object-oriented programming and how to apply them effectively in your projects.

CHAPTER 5

METHODS AND FUNCTIONS IN JAVA

Methods are a fundamental concept in Java programming that allow you to organize your code into reusable blocks. In this chapter, we will explore how to define and call methods, use method parameters and return types, implement method overloading, and understand recursion through recursive methods.

Method Definition and Calling Methods

1. **Method Definition**: A method in Java is a block of code that performs a specific task. It is defined inside a class and can be called (or invoked) from other parts of the program. A method consists of:

    o **Method signature**: Includes the method's name, return type, and parameters.

    o **Method body**: Contains the statements that define what the method does.

Syntax for defining a method:

```java
```

48

```
returnType           methodName(parameter1,
parameter2, ...) {
    // Method body
    // Code to be executed
}
```

Example:

```java
public class MathOperations {
    // Method to add two integers
    public int add(int num1, int num2) {
        return num1 + num2;
    }
}
```

Here, `add` is a method that takes two integers as parameters and returns their sum as an integer. The method has a return type of `int`.

2. **Calling a Method**: Once a method is defined, you can call it from other parts of your program by using its name and providing the necessary arguments for the parameters.

Example:

```java
java

public class Main {
    public static void main(String[] args)
{
        MathOperations    math    =    new
MathOperations(); // Create an object of
MathOperations class
        int result = math.add(5, 3);   //
Calling the add method
        System.out.println("The sum is: "
+ result);  // Output: The sum is: 8
    }
}
```

Here, `math.add(5, 3)` calls the `add` method from the `MathOperations` class, passing the values 5 and 3 as arguments.

Method Parameters and Return Types

1. **Method Parameters**: Parameters are variables that are passed to a method to provide input values. A method can have zero or more parameters, which are specified in the method definition.

- o **Example**: A method that calculates the area of a rectangle requires the length and width as input parameters:

```java
public double calculateArea(double
length, double width) {
    return length * width;
}
```

2. When calling the method, you provide actual values for these parameters:
3. java
4.
5. double area = calculateArea(5.0, 3.0); // Output will be 15.0
6. **Return Types**: A return type specifies the type of value a method will return after its execution. Methods can return values of any data type (e.g., int, double, String, or even custom types). If a method does not return a value, its return type is specified as void.

- o **Example of a method with a return type**:

```java
public int multiply(int a, int b) {
    return a * b;  // Returns the
product of a and b
```

```
}
```

- o **Example of a method with void return type**:

```java
public    void    printMessage(String
message) {
    System.out.println(message);   //
This method does not return any value
}
```

Method Overloading and Its Real-World Use Case

1. **What is Method Overloading?**
   Method overloading is a feature in Java that allows you to define multiple methods with the same name but different parameters. This helps to perform similar tasks with different types or numbers of inputs.

   The Java compiler differentiates between the overloaded methods based on the number or types of parameters passed to them.

2. **Syntax for Method Overloading**: The method signature (method name and parameter list) must be different for each overloaded method.

Example of method overloading:

java

```java
public class Calculator {
    // Overloaded method to add two
integers
    public int add(int num1, int num2) {
        return num1 + num2;
    }

    // Overloaded method to add three
integers
    public int add(int num1, int num2, int
num3) {
        return num1 + num2 + num3;
    }

    // Overloaded method to add two doubles
    public double add(double num1, double
num2) {
        return num1 + num2;
    }
}
```

In this example, the add method is overloaded with three different signatures:

o   Adding two integers.

- o Adding three integers.
- o Adding two doubles.

Calling overloaded methods:

```java
public class Main {
    public static void main(String[] args) {
        Calculator calc = new Calculator();
        System.out.println("Sum of 2 numbers: " + calc.add(5, 3));  // Calls add(int, int)
        System.out.println("Sum of 3 numbers: " + calc.add(1, 2, 3)); // Calls add(int, int, int)
        System.out.println("Sum of 2 doubles: " + calc.add(2.5, 3.7)); // Calls add(double, double)
    }
}
```

Real-World Use Case of Method Overloading: Method overloading is commonly used in scenarios where you want to perform the same action but with different types of inputs. For example:

- In a **calculator program**, you may want to provide methods for adding both integers and decimals.
- In a **logging system**, you might want to log messages in different formats: one for error messages, and another for general info messages.

Recursive Methods with Examples

1. **What is Recursion?**
   Recursion is a technique where a method calls itself to solve a smaller instance of the same problem. The method must have a **base case** to stop the recursion and prevent infinite calls.

2. **Example of a Recursive Method**: A common example of recursion is calculating the **factorial** of a number. The factorial of a number n is the product of all positive integers less than or equal to n. For example, 5! = 5 * 4 * 3 * 2 * 1 = 120.

Factorial Method (recursive):

```java
public class MathOperations {
    public int factorial(int n) {
        if (n == 0) {   // Base case
```

```
        return 1;
      } else {
        return n * factorial(n - 1);
// Recursive call
      }
    }
}
```

How it works:

- The method calls itself with a smaller value of n until it reaches the base case (n == 0).
- When n == 0, the method returns 1, which then allows all the previous calls to return their values.

Calling the factorial method:

java

```
public class Main {
    public static void main(String[] args) {
        MathOperations math = new MathOperations();
        int result = math.factorial(5);
        System.out.println("Factorial of 5: " + result);  // Output: 120
    }
}
```

3. **Real-World Example of Recursion**: Recursion is often used in problems involving hierarchical structures, such as:

   o **Tree traversals** (e.g., in binary trees or file systems).

   o **Fibonacci sequence** calculation, where each term is the sum of the two preceding ones.

Example of calculating Fibonacci numbers:

java

```java
public class MathOperations {
    public int fibonacci(int n) {
        if (n <= 1) {  // Base case
            return n;
        } else {
            return  fibonacci(n  -  1)  +
fibonacci(n - 2);  // Recursive call
        }
    }
}
```

Summary

In this chapter, we covered essential concepts related to methods and functions in Java:

- **Method Definition and Calling**: We learned how to define and call methods to perform specific tasks in a Java program.

- **Method Parameters and Return Types**: We explored how methods can accept input parameters and return values, and the significance of the `void` return type.

- **Method Overloading**: We examined how Java allows methods with the same name but different parameter lists, making it easier to perform similar operations with different inputs.

- **Recursive Methods**: We looked at recursion as a method calling itself to solve problems and how it is useful in solving problems like calculating factorials or Fibonacci numbers.

With these concepts in place, you are now equipped to write efficient and modular Java programs using methods to organize your code. In the next chapters, we will continue to build on these principles and dive deeper into more advanced Java features.

CHAPTER 6

UNDERSTANDING JAVA INHERITANCE

Inheritance is one of the core principles of Object-Oriented Programming (OOP). It allows you to create a new class based on an existing class, enabling code reuse and establishing a relationship between the new class and the existing one. In this chapter, we will explore the concept of inheritance, how to create and use subclasses, and the role of the `extends` keyword in Java. We will also look at practical real-world examples where inheritance is applied.

Concept of Inheritance in OOP

In Object-Oriented Programming, **inheritance** is a mechanism where one class (called the **subclass** or **child class**) inherits the fields and methods of another class (called the **superclass** or **parent class**). This helps in reusing code and establishing relationships between classes in a hierarchical manner.

- **Superclass**: The class whose properties and methods are inherited by the subclass.

- **Subclass**: The class that inherits the properties and methods of the superclass.

Inheritance allows a subclass to have all the attributes and behaviors of the superclass while adding its own unique attributes and behaviors. This promotes the **DRY principle** (Don't Repeat Yourself), reducing the need for redundant code.

Creating and Using Subclasses

To create a subclass in Java, you use the `extends` keyword, followed by the name of the class you want to inherit from. The subclass inherits all non-private members (fields and methods) of the superclass, and you can also add new members or override inherited methods to modify or extend their functionality.

1. **Creating a Subclass**: In Java, the subclass inherits the members of the superclass, but it cannot inherit the constructor of the superclass. However, the subclass can call the superclass constructor using the `super()` keyword.

   Syntax for creating a subclass:

   ```java
   java

   public class Superclass {
   ```

```java
    // Fields
    String name;

    // Constructor
    public Superclass(String name) {
        this.name = name;
    }

    // Method
    public void display() {
        System.out.println("Name:    "    +
name);
    }
}

public class Subclass extends Superclass {
    // Additional fields
    int age;

    // Constructor
    public Subclass(String name, int age)
{
        super(name);    // Call to the
superclass constructor
        this.age = age;
    }

    // Additional method
    public void showAge() {
```

```
        System.out.println("Age: " + age);
    }
}
```

2. **Using the Subclass**: Now that we have defined the subclass, you can create an object of the subclass and call both the inherited and new methods.

java

```
public class Main {
    public static void main(String[] args)
{
        // Creating an object of Subclass
        Subclass    person    =    new
Subclass("John", 30);
        person.display();    // Inherited
from Superclass
        person.showAge();    // Defined in
Subclass
    }
}
```

Output:

makefile

```
Name: John
Age: 30
```

In this example:

- o `person.display()` calls the `display()` method from the superclass `Superclass`.
- o `person.showAge()` calls the `showAge()` method from the subclass `Subclass`.

The `extends` Keyword and Its Practical Use

The `extends` keyword is used to establish an inheritance relationship between two classes. By using `extends`, the subclass inherits the public and protected members (fields and methods) of the superclass.

- **The extends keyword** is placed between the subclass and the superclass to create a subclass:

java

```
public class Subclass extends Superclass {
    // Subclass code here
}
```

1. **Accessing Superclass Members**: Once the subclass extends the superclass, it can access the inherited members (fields and methods) of the superclass, provided those members are accessible (public or protected).

2. **Constructor Inheritance**: The subclass does not inherit the constructor of the superclass. However, it can call the superclass constructor using the `super()` keyword.

   o **Calling the superclass constructor**:

   java

   ```java
   public class Subclass extends
   Superclass {
       public Subclass(String name) {
           super(name);  // Calls the
   constructor of the superclass
       }
   }
   ```

3. **Overriding Methods**: A subclass can **override** methods from the superclass to provide its own implementation. This is done by using the `@Override` annotation.

   Example:

   java

   ```java
   public class Superclass {
       public void greet() {
           System.out.println("Hello from the
   superclass!");
       }
   }
   ```

```java
public class Subclass extends Superclass {
    @Override
    public void greet() {
        System.out.println("Hello from the
subclass!");
    }
}
```

When we create an object of the subclass and call the greet() method, the subclass's version of the method is invoked, not the superclass's version:

java

```java
Subclass obj = new Subclass();
obj.greet();    // Output: Hello from the
subclass!
```

Real-World Examples of Inheritance

1. **Employee -> Manager**: Consider a real-world analogy where Employee is the superclass, and Manager is a subclass. An employee has general attributes like name, salary, and position, while a manager has additional responsibilities, such as managing teams.

   Superclass (Employee):

java

```java
public class Employee {
    String name;
    double salary;

    public Employee(String name, double salary) {
        this.name = name;
        this.salary = salary;
    }

    public void displayInfo() {
        System.out.println("Name:    " + name);
        System.out.println("Salary:    " + salary);
    }
}
```

Subclass (Manager):

java

```java
public class Manager extends Employee {
    String department;

    public Manager(String name, double salary, String department) {
```

```
        super(name, salary);   // Calls the
Employee constructor
        this.department = department;
    }

    public void displayDepartment() {
        System.out.println("Department:   "
+ department);
    }

    @Override
    public void displayInfo() {
        super.displayInfo();   // Calls the
Employee's displayInfo method
        System.out.println("Department:   "
+ department);
    }
}
```

Using the Classes:

```java
java

public class Main {
    public static void main(String[] args)
{
        Manager    manager    =    new
Manager("Alice", 85000, "HR");
```

```
        manager.displayInfo();              //
Displays  Employee's  info  and  Manager's
department
    }
}
```

Output:

```
makefile


Name: Alice
Salary: 85000.0
Department: HR
```

In this example:

- o `Manager` extends `Employee` and adds an extra field, `department`.
- o The `Manager` class overrides the `displayInfo()` method to include the department information.

2. **Vehicle -> Car**: Another real-world analogy is the relationship between `Vehicle` and `Car`. A `Vehicle` is a general class with properties such as `speed` and `fuel`, while a `Car` extends `Vehicle` and adds specific attributes like `numberOfDoors`.

Superclass (Vehicle):

```java
java

public class Vehicle {
    int speed;
    int fuel;

    public Vehicle(int speed, int fuel) {
        this.speed = speed;
        this.fuel = fuel;
    }

    public void drive() {
        System.out.println("Driving      at
speed: " + speed);
    }
}
```

Subclass (Car):

```java
java

public class Car extends Vehicle {
    int numberOfDoors;

    public Car(int speed, int fuel, int
numberOfDoors) {
        super(speed, fuel);
        this.numberOfDoors                =
numberOfDoors;
    }
```

```java
    @Override
    public void drive() {
        super.drive();  // Calls Vehicle's drive method
        System.out.println("Number        of doors: " + numberOfDoors);
    }
}
```

Using the Classes:

java

```java
public class Main {
    public static void main(String[] args) {
        Car car = new Car(120, 50, 4);
        car.drive();  // Displays the speed and number of doors of the car
    }
}
```

Output:

yaml

```
Driving at speed: 120
Number of doors: 4
```

In this example:

- o `Car` extends `Vehicle` and adds a new attribute, `numberOfDoors`.
- o The `drive()` method is overridden in the `Car` class to add additional functionality.

Summary

In this chapter, we've explored:

- **The concept of inheritance**: A mechanism that allows a class to inherit the properties and behaviors of another class.
- **Creating and using subclasses**: Subclasses inherit fields and methods from the superclass and can also define their own properties and methods.
- **The `extends` keyword**: This keyword is used to establish inheritance between a superclass and a subclass.
- **Real-world examples**: We used real-world analogies like `Employee -> Manager` and `Vehicle -> Car` to demonstrate how inheritance works and how it can model relationships between objects in Java.

Inheritance is a powerful concept that makes your Java code more modular and reusable. In the next chapters, we will dive deeper into other key object-oriented principles like polymorphism, encapsulation, and abstraction.

CHAPTER 7

POLYMORPHISM IN JAVA

Polymorphism is one of the most powerful and essential features of Object-Oriented Programming (OOP). It allows objects to be treated as instances of their parent class, enabling a high level of flexibility and reusability in code. In this chapter, we will explore what polymorphism is, why it is important in OOP, the difference between overriding and overloading, and the concepts of runtime and compile-time polymorphism. We will also provide a real-world example using an `Animal` class with different species like `Dog` and `Cat`.

What is Polymorphism and Why It's Important in OOP?

Polymorphism is derived from the Greek words *poly* (meaning "many") and *morph* (meaning "form"). In programming, polymorphism refers to the ability of an object to take on many forms. It allows you to use a single interface or method to represent different underlying forms (data types). This is an essential feature of OOP because it enhances code flexibility, reusability, and maintainability.

There are two main types of polymorphism in Java:

- **Compile-time Polymorphism (Static Binding)**
- **Runtime Polymorphism (Dynamic Binding)**

The main benefit of polymorphism is that it allows for a more generalized approach to handling objects. You can create a method or class that works with any subclass of a particular superclass, enabling flexibility and reducing the need for code duplication.

Overriding vs. Overloading

Polymorphism in Java can be achieved in two ways: **method overriding** and **method overloading**. Let's explore both concepts:

1. **Method Overriding**: Method overriding occurs when a subclass provides a specific implementation of a method that is already defined in its superclass. The overridden method in the subclass must have the same name, return type, and parameters as the method in the superclass. Overriding allows a subclass to alter or extend the behavior of an inherited method.

   o **Why is it important?** Overriding is useful because it allows a subclass to provide its specific behavior while maintaining

74

the same method signature, thus enabling polymorphism.

Example of Method Overriding:

java

```java
public class Animal {
    public void sound() {
        System.out.println("The    animal
makes a sound.");
    }
}


public class Dog extends Animal {
    @Override
    public void sound() {
        System.out.println("The    dog
barks.");
    }
}


public class Cat extends Animal {
    @Override
    public void sound() {
        System.out.println("The    cat
meows.");
    }
}
```

```java
public class Main {
    public static void main(String[] args)
{
        Animal myAnimal = new Animal();
        myAnimal.sound();   // Output: The
animal makes a sound.

        Animal myDog = new Dog();
        myDog.sound();   // Output: The dog
barks.

        Animal myCat = new Cat();
        myCat.sound();   // Output: The cat
meows.
    }
}
```

In this example, the sound() method is overridden in both the Dog and Cat subclasses. The actual method called depends on the object type (runtime polymorphism).

2. **Method Overloading**: Method overloading occurs when multiple methods with the same name are defined in the same class, but with different parameters. The methods can differ by the number or type of parameters. This is known as compile-time polymorphism because the

method to be called is determined at compile time based on the method signature.

- o **Why is it important?** Overloading allows you to use the same method name to perform similar tasks with different types or numbers of arguments, enhancing readability and reusability.

Example of Method Overloading:

java

```java
public class Calculator {
    // Method to add two integers
    public int add(int a, int b) {
        return a + b;
    }

    // Overloaded method to add three
integers
    public int add(int a, int b, int c) {
        return a + b + c;
    }

    // Overloaded method to add two doubles
    public double add(double a, double b)
{
        return a + b;
    }
```

```
}

public class Main {
    public static void main(String[] args)
{
        Calculator    calc    =    new
Calculator();
        System.out.println(calc.add(5,
3));   // Output: 8
        System.out.println(calc.add(1,   2,
3));   // Output: 6
        System.out.println(calc.add(5.5,
4.5));   // Output: 10.0
    }
}
```

In this example, the add() method is overloaded with different parameter types and counts. The appropriate method is selected at compile time based on the arguments provided.

Runtime and Compile-time Polymorphism

1. **Compile-Time Polymorphism** (Static Binding): Compile-time polymorphism is also known as **method overloading**. It is resolved during the compilation phase, where the method to be invoked is determined based on the method signature (number and type of parameters). In

method overloading, the method to be called is decided at compile time.

Example: In the previous section, the `add()` method in the `Calculator` class is overloaded with different parameters. The correct method is determined during the compilation phase.

2. **Runtime Polymorphism** (Dynamic Binding): Runtime polymorphism, also known as **method overriding**, occurs when a method is called on an object, and the method that gets executed is determined at runtime based on the actual object type, not the reference type. This allows for more flexible and dynamic behavior in object-oriented programs.

   Example: In the animal example above, the method `sound()` is overridden in both the `Dog` and `Cat` classes. Even though the reference is of type `Animal`, the actual method that is called (bark or meow) depends on the type of the object (Dog or Cat) at runtime. This is a classic example of runtime polymorphism.

Real-World Example: Animal Class with Different Species (Dog, Cat)

Let's dive deeper into a real-world analogy using the **Animal** class and its subclasses (Dog, Cat).

1. **Superclass (Animal):**

java

```java
public class Animal {
    public void sound() {
        System.out.println("The     animal makes a sound.");
    }
}
```

2. **Subclass (Dog):**

java

```java
public class Dog extends Animal {
    @Override
    public void sound() {
        System.out.println("The     dog barks.");
    }
}
```

3. **Subclass (Cat):**

80

java

```java
public class Cat extends Animal {
    @Override
    public void sound() {
        System.out.println("The          cat
meows.");
    }
}
```

4. **Using Polymorphism**:

java

```java
public class Main {
    public static void main(String[] args)
{
        Animal myAnimal = new Animal();
        myAnimal.sound();   // Output: The
animal makes a sound.

        Animal myDog = new Dog();
        myDog.sound();   // Output: The dog
barks.

        Animal myCat = new Cat();
        myCat.sound();   // Output: The cat
meows.
    }
}
```

In the above example, we have a superclass `Animal` with a method `sound()`. Both the `Dog` and `Cat` classes override the `sound()` method to provide their own implementations. Even though the reference type is `Animal`, the actual method that gets called depends on the runtime type of the object (either `Dog` or `Cat`). This is **runtime polymorphism**.

Key points:

- o **Method Overriding** (runtime polymorphism): The actual method executed depends on the object type, not the reference type.
- o **Method Overloading** (compile-time polymorphism): The method to be executed is determined at compile time based on the method signature.

Summary

In this chapter, we have covered the following key concepts:

- **Polymorphism**: The ability of an object to take on many forms. It allows for flexibility and reusability in code.
- **Overriding vs. Overloading**: Overriding occurs when a subclass provides a specific implementation of a

superclass method, while overloading happens when multiple methods share the same name but differ in parameters.

- **Compile-time Polymorphism**: Achieved through method overloading, where the method to be called is resolved at compile time.

- **Runtime Polymorphism**: Achieved through method overriding, where the method to be called is determined at runtime based on the actual object type.

Polymorphism is a powerful feature in Java that helps you write flexible, reusable, and maintainable code. By leveraging polymorphism, you can design systems that are easier to extend and modify. In the next chapters, we will continue to explore other key OOP principles like abstraction and encapsulation, further enhancing your ability to write efficient Java programs.

CHAPTER 8

ABSTRACTION IN JAVA

Abstraction is a fundamental concept in Object-Oriented Programming (OOP), and it is crucial for simplifying complex systems by focusing on the essential characteristics while hiding unnecessary implementation details. In this chapter, we will explore what abstraction is, the difference between abstract classes and interfaces, how to create and use abstract classes and methods, and provide a real-world analogy to help visualize abstraction in action.

What is Abstraction?

Abstraction is the process of hiding the complex implementation details of a system and exposing only the essential features to the user. In Java, abstraction allows you to define the structure of your classes without specifying the exact details of how they will function. This is typically done by using **abstract classes** or **interfaces**, which provide templates for other classes to implement.

By using abstraction, you can design cleaner, more manageable code. It lets you focus on what a system does, rather than how it does it. This reduces complexity and allows for better maintenance and extensibility of your code.

Abstract Classes vs. Interfaces

In Java, there are two main ways to achieve abstraction: **abstract classes** and **interfaces**. Both of them are used to provide a blueprint for other classes to follow, but they differ in several key ways:

1. **Abstract Classes**:
    - An **abstract class** cannot be instantiated, meaning you cannot create an object of the abstract class directly. It is meant to be extended by other classes.
    - An abstract class can have both **abstract methods** (methods without a body) and **concrete methods** (methods with a body).
    - It may also contain fields, constructors, and methods that can be inherited by subclasses.
    - Abstract methods must be implemented by the subclasses, but concrete methods may be inherited as-is or overridden.

Syntax for Abstract Class:

```java
```

85

```java
public abstract class Animal {
    // Abstract method (does not have a body)
    public abstract void sound();

    // Concrete method
    public void sleep() {
        System.out.println("This animal is sleeping.");
    }
}
```

- o **Abstract method**: A method that is declared without an implementation. Subclasses must provide their own implementation of this method.
- o **Concrete method**: A method that has a complete implementation. Subclasses can either use it as-is or override it.

2. **Interfaces**:

- o An **interface** is a reference type in Java, similar to a class, but it can contain only **abstract methods** (methods without a body) and **static final variables** (constants). Interfaces cannot have instance fields or constructors.
- o A class can implement multiple interfaces, allowing for more flexibility than abstract classes (which support single inheritance).

86

    o   The methods in an interface must be implemented by the classes that implement the interface.

Syntax for Interface:

java

```java
public interface Animal {
    // Abstract method (does not have a
body)
    void sound();

    // Interface can only have constants
(final variables)
    int numberOfLegs = 4;   // default is
static and final
}
```

    o   **Implementation of an Interface**: A class that implements an interface must provide implementations for all the abstract methods in the interface.

java

```java
public class Dog implements Animal {
    @Override
    public void sound() {
        System.out.println("Bark");
```

87

```
        }
    }
```

Creating and Using Abstract Classes and Methods

1. **Abstract Classes**:
    o You define an abstract class using the `abstract` keyword.
    o Abstract methods in an abstract class must be implemented by its subclasses unless the subclass is also abstract.

Example: Abstract Class and Method:

java

```java
public abstract class Shape {
    // Abstract method
    public abstract double area();
}

public class Circle extends Shape {
    private double radius;

    public Circle(double radius) {
        this.radius = radius;
    }
```

```java
    // Implementing the abstract method
    @Override
    public double area() {
        return Math.PI * radius * radius;
    }
}


public class Rectangle extends Shape {
    private double length;
    private double width;

    public Rectangle(double length, double
width) {
        this.length = length;
        this.width = width;
    }


    // Implementing the abstract method
    @Override
    public double area() {
        return length * width;
    }
}

public class Main {
    public static void main(String[] args)
{
        Shape circle = new Circle(5);
```

```
        System.out.println("Area        of
circle: " + circle.area());

        Shape rectangle = new Rectangle(4,
6);
        System.out.println("Area        of
rectangle: " + rectangle.area());
    }
}
```

In this example:

- o The **Shape** class is abstract and contains an abstract method `area()`.
- o The **Circle** and **Rectangle** classes are concrete classes that extend `Shape` and provide their own implementation of the `area()` method.

Output:

yaml

```
Area of circle: 78.53981633974483
Area of rectangle: 24.0
```

2. **Abstract Methods**:
   - o An abstract method in an abstract class must be implemented by any non-abstract subclass. This ensures that subclasses provide specific behavior

for methods that have no default implementation in the abstract class.

Example:

```java

public abstract class Animal {
    public abstract void sound();    // Abstract method

    public void eat() {
        System.out.println("This animal is eating.");
    }
}
```

Real-World Analogy: Abstract Class for a Vehicle and Concrete Subclasses

Let's consider a **Vehicle** as an abstract class. All vehicles share some basic characteristics (like speed and fuel), but the way they move is different for each type of vehicle (e.g., a **Car** moves differently than a **Bicycle**). By using abstraction, we can define the general structure in the `Vehicle` class and let the subclasses provide their own specific implementations.

1. **Abstract Class (Vehicle):**

91

java

```java
public abstract class Vehicle {
    String make;
    String model;

    // Constructor
    public Vehicle(String make, String model) {
        this.make = make;
        this.model = model;
    }

    // Abstract method
    public abstract void move();

    // Concrete method
    public void fuelUp() {
        System.out.println("Fueling up the vehicle.");
    }
}
```

2. **Concrete Subclass (Car):**

java

```java
public class Car extends Vehicle {
    int doors;
```

```java
    public Car(String make, String model,
int doors) {
        super(make, model);
        this.doors = doors;
    }

    @Override
    public void move() {
        System.out.println("The    car    is
driving.");
    }
}
```

3. **Concrete Subclass (Bicycle)**:

```
java
```

```java
public class Bicycle extends Vehicle {
    int gears;

    public  Bicycle(String  make,  String
model, int gears) {
        super(make, model);
        this.gears = gears;
    }

    @Override
    public void move() {
        System.out.println("The bicycle is
pedaling.");
```

93

```
    }
}
```

4. **Using the Classes**:

```java
public class Main {
    public static void main(String[] args)
{
        Vehicle myCar = new Car("Toyota",
"Camry", 4);
        myCar.move();   // Output: The car
is driving.
        myCar.fuelUp();         //   Output:
Fueling up the vehicle.

        Vehicle    myBicycle    =    new
Bicycle("Giant", "Escape", 21);
        myBicycle.move();   // Output: The
bicycle is pedaling.
        myBicycle.fuelUp();    //  Output:
Fueling up the vehicle.
    }
}
```

In this example:

- o The **Vehicle** class is abstract, providing a template for all vehicles.

94

o The **Car** and **Bicycle** classes are concrete subclasses that provide specific implementations for the `move()` method, which varies for each vehicle type.

Key Concepts:

o **Vehicle (abstract class)** provides a general blueprint for all vehicles, including an abstract method `move()` and a concrete method `fuelUp()`.

o **Car** and **Bicycle** are concrete subclasses that implement the `move()` method to define their own movement behaviors.

Summary

In this chapter, we have covered the following:

- **Abstraction**: The process of hiding complex details and exposing only the essential features of a system.
- **Abstract Classes vs. Interfaces**: We explored the differences between abstract classes (which can contain both abstract and concrete methods) and interfaces (which only contain abstract methods).

- **Creating and Using Abstract Classes**: We learned how to define and use abstract classes and methods, and how subclasses must implement abstract methods.

- **Real-World Analogy**: The `Vehicle` class and its subclasses (`Car`, `Bicycle`) served as a real-world analogy to demonstrate how abstraction can be used to model general concepts while allowing subclasses to define specific behaviors.

Abstraction is an essential concept in OOP, as it allows developers to define generic templates and allow subclasses to specialize their behavior. This helps to create modular, maintainable, and flexible systems. In the next chapters, we will explore other key OOP concepts such as **encapsulation** and **polymorphism**, which build upon the foundation of abstraction.

CHAPTER 9

ENCAPSULATION IN JAVA

Encapsulation is one of the core principles of Object-Oriented Programming (OOP). It allows for data protection by bundling the data (variables) and the methods that operate on the data within a single unit, called a **class**. Encapsulation also hides the internal details of the class, exposing only the necessary features. This chapter will dive into the concept of encapsulation, the use of access modifiers, getter and setter methods, and provide a real-world analogy using a bank account.

Understanding Encapsulation and Its Benefits

Encapsulation is the process of restricting access to the internal state of an object and only allowing external code to interact with the object through a well-defined interface (methods). This is done by marking class fields as **private** and providing **public** methods (getters and setters) to access and modify these fields.

The primary benefits of encapsulation include:

1. **Data Hiding**: By keeping fields private, the internal implementation is hidden from outside code. This

prevents unauthorized access and modification of the object's state.

2. **Improved Maintainability**: Encapsulation makes it easier to change the internal workings of a class without affecting external code. If the implementation of a method changes, as long as the interface (method signatures) remains the same, external code does not need to be modified.

3. **Better Control**: Getters and setters allow you to control how fields are accessed and modified. For example, you can validate inputs in setter methods to ensure that the data remains consistent and valid.

4. **Flexibility**: Encapsulation allows for the safe modification of a class's internals without breaking existing code. You can change the internal workings of the class without worrying about how it will impact other parts of the program.

Access Modifiers (private, protected, public)

In Java, **access modifiers** define the visibility and accessibility of classes, methods, and fields. There are four main access modifiers in Java:

1. **private**: The field or method is **only accessible within the same class**. It cannot be accessed directly from outside the class.

   o **Use**: To encapsulate data and prevent unauthorized access.

   Example:

   ```java
   ```

   ```java
   private int balance;
   ```

2. **protected**: The field or method is **accessible within the same package** and by subclasses (even if they are in different packages).

   o **Use**: To allow access to certain members by subclasses or classes within the same package.

   Example:

   ```java
   ```

   ```java
   protected String accountType;
   ```

3. **public**: The field or method is **accessible from anywhere** in the program.

   o **Use**: To expose methods or fields that should be accessible from other classes.

Example:

java

```
public void deposit(double amount) {
    // Deposit logic
}
```

4. **default** (no modifier): If no access modifier is specified, the field or method is **accessible within the same package**.

   o **Use**: To allow access to members within the same package without exposing them outside the package.

Example:

java

```
String    accountHolderName;    //    Default
access
```

Getter and Setter Methods

Getter methods (also known as **accessors**) are used to retrieve the value of a private field. **Setter methods** (also known as **mutators**) are used to modify the value of a private field.

Why use getters and setters?

- They allow controlled access to the fields of a class.
- They help in **data validation**. For example, you can check if a value is valid before assigning it to a field (e.g., ensuring an age is not negative).
- They can provide the flexibility to change how data is accessed or modified without changing the external interface of the class.

Example of Getter and Setter Methods:

java

```java
public class BankAccount {
    // Private fields (data encapsulation)
    private double balance;
    private String accountHolder;

    // Getter method for balance
    public double getBalance() {
        return balance;
    }

    // Setter method for balance
    public void setBalance(double balance) {
        if (balance >= 0) {  // Validation logic
            this.balance = balance;
        } else {
```

```
        System.out.println("Balance    cannot
be negative.");
        }
    }


    // Getter method for account holder
    public String getAccountHolder() {
        return accountHolder;
    }


    // Setter method for account holder
    public    void    setAccountHolder(String
accountHolder) {
        this.accountHolder = accountHolder;
    }
}
```

In this example:

- **getBalance()** is the getter method that returns the value of the balance field.
- **setBalance(double balance)** is the setter method that assigns a value to the balance field after validating that it is non-negative.
- **getAccountHolder()** and **setAccountHolder(String accountHolder)** are getter and setter methods for the accountHolder field.

Using Getter and Setter Methods:

java

```java
public class Main {
    public static void main(String[] args) {
        BankAccount    myAccount    =    new
BankAccount();

        // Set account details
        myAccount.setAccountHolder("John Doe");
        myAccount.setBalance(500.0);

        // Get account details
        System.out.println("Account  Holder:  " +
myAccount.getAccountHolder());
        System.out.println("Balance:    $"    +
myAccount.getBalance());
    }
}
```

Output:

yaml

```
Account Holder: John Doe
Balance: $500.0
```

By using getter and setter methods, we control how the data is accessed and modified, which helps in enforcing rules (like ensuring a balance can't be negative).

Real-World Analogy: Bank Account with Methods to Deposit and Withdraw

Let's consider a **BankAccount** class to demonstrate encapsulation in action. The BankAccount class will have a private field balance (which stores the account balance), and we'll provide methods to deposit money, withdraw money, and get the current balance.

1. **BankAccount Class** (with encapsulation):

java

```java
public class BankAccount {
    // Private field (encapsulation)
    private double balance;

    // Constructor to initialize balance
    public                  BankAccount(double
initialBalance) {
        if (initialBalance >= 0) {
            balance = initialBalance;
        } else {
            System.out.println("Initial
balance cannot be negative.");
            balance = 0;
        }
    }
```

```java
    // Method to deposit money
    public void deposit(double amount) {
        if (amount > 0) {
            balance += amount;

System.out.println("Deposited:    $"    +
amount);
        } else {
            System.out.println("Deposit
amount must be positive.");
        }
    }


    // Method to withdraw money
    public void withdraw(double amount) {
        if (amount > 0 && amount <=
balance) {
            balance -= amount;
            System.out.println("Withdrew:
$" + amount);
        } else {

System.out.println("Insufficient funds or
invalid amount.");
        }
    }

    // Getter method for balance
```

```java
    public double getBalance() {
        return balance;
    }
}
```

2. Using the BankAccount Class:

java

```java
public class Main {
    public static void main(String[] args)
{
        // Creating a new bank account with
an initial balance
        BankAccount    myAccount    =    new
BankAccount(1000.0);

        // Performing transactions
        myAccount.deposit(500.0);        //
Deposit $500
        myAccount.withdraw(300.0);       //
Withdraw $300
        myAccount.withdraw(1500.0);      //
Attempt to withdraw more than available
balance

        // Getting the balance
        System.out.println("Current
Balance: $" + myAccount.getBalance());
    }
```

```
}
```

Output:

```
pgsql

Deposited: $500.0
Withdrew: $300.0
Insufficient funds or invalid amount.
Current Balance: $1200.0
```

Key Points:

- o **Private Field**: `balance` is marked as private to protect it from direct access and modification.
- o **Public Methods**: `deposit()`, `withdraw()`, and `getBalance()` are public methods that interact with the private `balance` field.
- o **Validation**: The `deposit()` and `withdraw()` methods include validation to ensure that invalid or incorrect operations (e.g., negative deposits or insufficient funds) do not occur.

Summary

In this chapter, we've covered the following key concepts of **encapsulation** in Java:

- **Encapsulation**: The practice of bundling the data (fields) and the methods that operate on the data within a class, and restricting access to some of the object's components.

- **Access Modifiers**: The use of `private`, `protected`, and `public` access modifiers to control the visibility and accessibility of class members.

- **Getter and Setter Methods**: Methods that provide controlled access to private fields. Getters retrieve values, while setters modify them.

- **Real-World Analogy**: The `BankAccount` class demonstrates encapsulation by hiding the `balance` field and providing methods to interact with it, while ensuring data validity.

Encapsulation is a powerful feature in Java that promotes data integrity, reduces complexity, and improves maintainability by controlling access to an object's state. In the next chapters, we will continue to explore more advanced OOP principles like inheritance, polymorphism, and abstraction.

CHAPTER 10

JAVA EXCEPTION HANDLING

Exception handling is a critical part of Java programming. It allows you to handle runtime errors, making your programs more robust and preventing crashes. Java provides a powerful and flexible mechanism to deal with exceptions through **try-catch-finally** blocks. This chapter will explain what exceptions are, why they occur, how to handle them using try-catch blocks, how to throw exceptions, and how to create custom exceptions. We will also go through a real-world example of handling file reading exceptions.

What Are Exceptions and Why Do They Occur?

Exceptions in Java are unwanted or unexpected events that can disrupt the normal flow of a program. They occur during the execution of the program and can result in incorrect behavior or cause the program to terminate abruptly if not handled properly. Java provides a robust exception handling mechanism to address these issues without letting the program crash.

Why do exceptions occur?

- **Invalid user input**: For example, a program may expect a number, but the user inputs a string.

- **External factors**: For example, trying to read from a file that doesn't exist or accessing a database that is offline.

- **Logical errors**: Errors that occur when the program logic goes wrong, such as dividing a number by zero or accessing an array index that doesn't exist.

There are two main types of exceptions in Java:

1. **Checked exceptions**: These are exceptions that are checked at compile time. They typically represent external conditions (e.g., file not found, database unavailable).

2. **Unchecked exceptions**: These are exceptions that occur during runtime, often due to programming errors (e.g., `NullPointerException`, `ArrayIndexOutOfBoundsException`).

Try-Catch-Finally Blocks

In Java, exceptions are handled using a mechanism known as **try-catch**. The `try` block is used to enclose code that might throw an exception, and the `catch` block is used to handle the exception when it occurs. The `finally` block is optional, but it is used to execute important code (e.g., resource cleanup) regardless of whether an exception occurs or not.

1. **Try Block**: Encloses the code that might throw an exception.
2. **Catch Block**: Catches the exception and defines how to handle it.
3. **Finally Block**: This block is always executed, whether or not an exception occurs, and is typically used for cleanup activities (like closing files or database connections).

Syntax:

```java
java

try {
    // Code that may throw an exception
} catch (ExceptionType e) {
    // Code to handle the exception
} finally {
    // Code that always executes, regardless of
an exception
}
```

Example of Try-Catch-Finally:

```java
java

public class Example {
```

```java
public static void main(String[] args) {
    try {
        int result = 10 / 0;  // Division by zero throws ArithmeticException
    } catch (ArithmeticException e) {
        System.out.println("Error: Division by zero is not allowed.");
    } finally {
        System.out.println("This will always execute.");
    }
}
}
```

Output:

pgsql

Error: Division by zero is not allowed.
This will always execute.

- **Try Block**: The code 10 / 0 will throw an ArithmeticException.
- **Catch Block**: The exception is caught and handled, printing an error message.
- **Finally Block**: This block executes whether an exception occurred or not, ensuring that cleanup code runs.

Throwing Exceptions and Custom Exceptions

In Java, you can **throw** exceptions manually using the `throw` keyword. Throwing exceptions is useful when you want to signal that something went wrong, such as invalid input or an error condition.

Syntax for throwing an exception:

```java
throw new ExceptionType("Error message");
```

Example of Throwing an Exception:

```java
public class Example {
    public static void main(String[] args) {
        try {
            validateAge(-5);     // Trying to
validate an invalid age
        } catch (IllegalArgumentException e) {
            System.out.println(e.getMessage());
// Prints: Age cannot be negative.
        }
    }

    public static void validateAge(int age) {
```

```
        if (age < 0) {
            throw                          new
IllegalArgumentException("Age      cannot      be
negative.");
        }
        System.out.println("Age  is  valid:  "  +
age);
    }
}
```

Output:

```
nginx
```

```
Age cannot be negative.
```

In this example, we are manually throwing an IllegalArgumentException if the age is negative. The exception is caught and handled in the catch block, which prints the error message.

Creating Custom Exceptions: You can also create your own exception types by extending the Exception class or any of its subclasses.

Example of a Custom Exception:

```
java
```

```java
public class InvalidBalanceException extends
Exception {
    public        InvalidBalanceException(String
message) {
        super(message);
    }
}

public class BankAccount {
    private double balance;

    public BankAccount(double balance) {
        this.balance = balance;
    }

    public void withdraw(double amount) throws
InvalidBalanceException {
        if (amount > balance) {
            throw                           new
InvalidBalanceException("Insufficient funds for
withdrawal.");
        }
        balance -= amount;
    }
}

public class Main {
    public static void main(String[] args) {
```

```
        BankAccount        account        =        new
BankAccount(500);

        try {
            account.withdraw(600);  // Trying to
withdraw more than the balance
        } catch (InvalidBalanceException e) {
            System.out.println(e.getMessage());
// Output: Insufficient funds for withdrawal.
        }
    }
}
```

Output:

```
rust


Insufficient funds for withdrawal.
```

In this example, `InvalidBalanceException` is a custom exception that is thrown when a withdrawal request exceeds the available balance.

Real-World Example: Handling File Reading Exceptions

One common scenario where exceptions are frequently encountered is **file reading**. When working with files, various issues can arise, such as the file not being found, permission

116

issues, or other IO problems. Exception handling is essential to manage these situations gracefully.

Example of Handling File Reading Exceptions:

```java
import java.io.*;

public class FileReaderExample {
    public static void main(String[] args) {
        try {
            FileReader file = new FileReader("example.txt"); // Trying to open a file
            BufferedReader reader = new BufferedReader(file);
            String line;
            while ((line = reader.readLine()) != null) {
                System.out.println(line); // Print each line of the file
            }
            reader.close();
        } catch (FileNotFoundException e) {
            System.out.println("Error: The file was not found.");
        } catch (IOException e) {
```

```
        System.out.println("Error: There was
a problem reading the file.");
      } finally {
        System.out.println("File      reading
attempt completed.");
      }
   }
}
```

In this example:

- The `FileReader` and `BufferedReader` are used to read a file.
- **FileNotFoundException** is caught if the file doesn't exist or the path is incorrect.
- **IOException** is caught if there are any issues while reading the file.
- The `finally` block ensures that we print a message whether or not the file reading was successful, and can be used to close resources.

Summary

In this chapter, we have covered the key aspects of **Java Exception Handling**:

- **What are exceptions and why they occur**: Exceptions are runtime errors that can disrupt the normal flow of a program. They occur due to various reasons like invalid input, external issues, or logical errors.

- **Try-catch-finally blocks**: We learned how to handle exceptions using `try`, `catch`, and `finally` blocks. The `finally` block ensures that certain actions (like resource cleanup) are always executed, regardless of whether an exception occurs.

- **Throwing exceptions and custom exceptions**: We explored how to throw exceptions manually using the `throw` keyword and how to create custom exceptions by extending the `Exception` class.

- **Real-world example**: We demonstrated how exceptions can be handled when working with files, including handling common file reading errors like file not found or IO issues.

Proper exception handling ensures that your program can gracefully recover from errors, providing better user experience and more robust applications. In the next chapters, we will continue to explore advanced Java concepts to improve your programming skills.

CHAPTER 11

WORKING WITH COLLECTIONS IN JAVA

The **Collections Framework** in Java is a powerful and versatile set of classes and interfaces that allow you to store and manipulate groups of data. It provides a wide range of collection types to accommodate various needs, such as lists, sets, and maps. Understanding how to use collections effectively is a crucial part of mastering Java programming. In this chapter, we will explore the collections framework, focusing on the key interfaces and classes like **Lists**, **Sets**, and **Maps**, and provide insights into choosing the right collection for your needs. We will also compare **ArrayList** and **LinkedList** and explore a real-world use case of storing student records.

Introduction to Collections Framework

The **Java Collections Framework** provides a set of interfaces, classes, and algorithms for working with data collections (groups of objects). It simplifies working with data structures and algorithms, allowing developers to focus on the problem at hand rather than implementing the underlying data structures.

Key components of the collections framework include:

1. **Interfaces**: Define the behavior of collections (e.g., `List`, `Set`, `Map`).

2. **Classes**: Provide concrete implementations of the collection interfaces (e.g., `ArrayList`, `HashSet`, `HashMap`).

3. **Algorithms**: Methods to perform operations like sorting, searching, and shuffling on collections (e.g., `Collections.sort()`).

Java collections are generally divided into three main categories:

- **Lists**: Ordered collections that allow duplicates.
- **Sets**: Unordered collections that do not allow duplicates.
- **Maps**: Key-value pairs for storing data with unique keys.

Lists, Sets, and Maps

1. **Lists**: A `List` is an ordered collection that allows duplicate elements. Elements in a `List` can be accessed by their position (index) in the list. The `List` interface is implemented by classes like `ArrayList`, `LinkedList`, and `Vector`.

   Key operations:

121

- o **Adding elements**: add()
- o **Accessing elements**: get()
- o **Removing elements**: remove()
- o **Size of the list**: size()

Example:

java

```
List<String> students = new ArrayList<>();
students.add("Alice");
students.add("Bob");
students.add("Charlie");
System.out.println(students.get(1));    //
Output: Bob
```

2. **Sets**: A Set is a collection that does not allow duplicate elements. It is unordered, meaning the elements have no guaranteed order. The Set interface is implemented by classes like HashSet, TreeSet, and LinkedHashSet.

Key operations:

- o **Adding elements**: add()
- o **Checking if an element exists**: contains()
- o **Removing elements**: remove()

Example:

```java

Set<String>    uniqueStudents    =    new
HashSet<>();
uniqueStudents.add("Alice");
uniqueStudents.add("Bob");
uniqueStudents.add("Alice");              //
Duplicate, will not be added
System.out.println(uniqueStudents);       //
Output: [Alice, Bob]
```

3. **Maps**: A `Map` is a collection that stores key-value pairs. Each key is unique, and each key maps to exactly one value. The `Map` interface is implemented by classes like `HashMap`, `TreeMap`, and `LinkedHashMap`.

   Key operations:

   - **Adding key-value pairs**: `put()`
   - **Accessing values by key**: `get()`
   - **Removing entries**: `remove()`

   Example:

```java

Map<String, Integer> studentGrades = new
HashMap<>();
studentGrades.put("Alice", 90);
```

123

```
studentGrades.put("Bob", 85);
System.out.println(studentGrades.get("Ali
ce")); // Output: 90
```

ArrayList vs. LinkedList

`ArrayList` and `LinkedList` are two popular implementations of the `List` interface in Java, but they have different internal structures and performance characteristics. Understanding the differences between them helps you choose the right implementation based on your use case.

1. **ArrayList**:
   - **Internal structure**: An `ArrayList` is backed by an array. It provides fast access to elements by index because arrays allow constant-time access (`O(1)`).
   - **Resizing**: When the array fills up, `ArrayList` automatically resizes, which can be an expensive operation (`O(n)`).
   - **Insertions and deletions**: Adding or removing elements at the end is generally fast (`O(1)`), but inserting or removing elements in the middle can be slow (`O(n)`), as all subsequent elements need to be shifted.

When to use: `ArrayList` is ideal for scenarios where you need fast random access to elements, and the number of insertions and deletions is relatively low.

2. **LinkedList**:

   o **Internal structure**: A `LinkedList` is backed by a doubly linked list, where each element points to the previous and next elements. It allows efficient insertions and deletions at both ends.

   o **Access time**: Accessing elements by index is slower than in `ArrayList` ($O(n)$), as it requires traversing the list.

   o **Insertions and deletions**: Adding or removing elements from the beginning or middle of the list is fast ($O(1)$), making it suitable for use cases where frequent insertions and deletions are required.

When to use: `LinkedList` is ideal when you need efficient insertion and deletion at both ends, or when the list will undergo frequent modifications.

Example of ArrayList and LinkedList:

java

```java
List<String> arrayList = new ArrayList<>();
arrayList.add("Alice");
```

```
arrayList.add("Bob");

List<String> linkedList = new LinkedList<>();
linkedList.add("Charlie");
linkedList.add("David");

System.out.println(arrayList.get(0));        //
Output: Alice
System.out.println(linkedList.get(1));       //
Output: David
```

Real-World Use Case: Storing Student Records in a List

Let's consider a **Student** class where each student has a name, ID, and grade. We will use a `List` to store student records and demonstrate how to add, access, and modify student data.

1. **Student Class**:

    ```java
    public class Student {
        private String name;
        private int id;
        private double grade;

        // Constructor
        public Student(String name, int id,
    double grade) {
    ```

```java
        this.name = name;
        this.id = id;
        this.grade = grade;
    }

    // Getter methods
    public String getName() {
        return name;
    }

    public int getId() {
        return id;
    }

    public double getGrade() {
        return grade;
    }

    // Display student details
    public void display() {
        System.out.println("ID: " + id + ",
Name: " + name + ", Grade: " + grade);
    }
}
```

2. **Using ArrayList to Store Student Records**:

```java
java

import java.util.ArrayList;
```

127

```java
import java.util.List;

public class Main {
    public static void main(String[] args)
{
        // Create a List to store student
records
        List<Student>    students   =   new
ArrayList<>();

        // Adding students to the list
        students.add(new  Student("Alice",
1, 90.5));
        students.add(new Student("Bob", 2,
85.3));
        students.add(new
Student("Charlie", 3, 92.0));

        //   Accessing   and   displaying
student records
        for (Student student : students) {
            student.display();
        }
    }
}
```

Output:

yaml

128

```
ID: 1, Name: Alice, Grade: 90.5
ID: 2, Name: Bob, Grade: 85.3
ID: 3, Name: Charlie, Grade: 92.0
```

In this example:

- We define a `Student` class with properties like `name`, `id`, and `grade`.
- We use an `ArrayList` to store multiple `Student` objects.
- We then iterate over the list using a `for-each` loop to access and display each student's information.

This demonstrates a common use case where a `List` is used to store and manage a collection of objects (students in this case), making it easier to perform operations like adding new records, retrieving specific data, or modifying existing records.

Summary

In this chapter, we covered the following aspects of working with collections in Java:

- **Introduction to the Collections Framework**: A powerful set of classes and interfaces to store and manipulate data.

- **Lists, Sets, and Maps**: We explored these three main types of collections and their operations.

- **ArrayList vs. LinkedList**: We compared the two most commonly used `List` implementations, highlighting when to use each.

- **Real-World Use Case**: We demonstrated how to store and manage student records using an `ArrayList`.

Understanding when and how to use different types of collections is essential for writing efficient and scalable Java programs. In the next chapters, we will continue to explore more advanced Java concepts and how they can be applied in real-world scenarios.

CHAPTER 12

GENERICS IN JAVA

Generics are a powerful feature in Java that allow you to write flexible and reusable code while maintaining strong type safety. By using generics, you can define classes, methods, and interfaces that can operate on any data type, yet still enforce type constraints at compile time. In this chapter, we will explore what generics are, how they improve type safety, how to create and use generic classes and methods, and how to work with wildcards and bounded types in generics. We will also provide a real-world analogy using a generic container for different types of objects.

What Are Generics and How Do They Improve Type Safety?

Generics enable you to write classes, methods, and interfaces that work with **any type** of data while preserving **type safety**. This means that you can create a class or method that can operate on any data type, but at compile time, Java ensures that the operations are performed safely, with no risk of type mismatches.

Before generics were introduced in Java, the collection classes (like `ArrayList`, `HashMap`, etc.) could hold elements of any type. However, this led to potential issues, as you could add objects of an incorrect type to the collection, leading to runtime errors.

With generics, you can specify the **type parameter** when defining a collection or method. This ensures that only the correct type of objects can be stored or operated upon, preventing errors and improving type safety.

Example of using generics without type safety:

java

```
List list = new ArrayList();
list.add("Hello");
list.add(5);   // Mixing different types
String str = (String) list.get(1);   // Runtime
error, casting an integer to String
```

Example of using generics with type safety:

java

```
List<String> list = new ArrayList<>();
list.add("Hello");
//   list.add(5);      //   Compile-time   error:
incompatible types
String str = list.get(0);   // Safe, no need for
casting
```

In the second example, the compiler ensures that only `String` objects can be added to the list. This reduces the risk of errors and improves the reliability of the code.

Creating and Using Generic Classes and Methods

1. **Generic Classes**: A **generic class** is a class that can operate on different types of data, and you specify the data type as a parameter when creating an object of the class. You define a generic class by using angle brackets (< >) with a type parameter.

   Syntax for defining a generic class:

   ```java
   public class Box<T> {
       private T value;

       public void setValue(T value) {
           this.value = value;
       }

       public T getValue() {
           return value;
       }
   }
   ```

In this example:

- o   T is the **type parameter**, which represents the data type that will be specified when creating an object of the class.
- o   The class Box has methods setValue() and getValue() that allow storing and retrieving the value of the specified type T.

Using the generic class:

java

```
public class Main {
    public static void main(String[] args)
{
        Box<String>    stringBox    =    new
Box<>();
        stringBox.setValue("Hello");

System.out.println(stringBox.getValue());
// Output: Hello

        Box<Integer> intBox = new Box<>();
        intBox.setValue(123);

System.out.println(intBox.getValue());   //
Output: 123
    }
```

134

```
}
```

In this example, we create two instances of the Box class, one for String and one for Integer, demonstrating how the class can work with different types while maintaining type safety.

2. **Generic Methods**: You can also define methods that use generics. This allows you to create reusable methods that can operate on different types of data.

   Syntax for defining a generic method:

```java

public <T> void printValue(T value) {
    System.out.println(value);
}
```

   In this example:

   - <T> before the return type void indicates that this method is generic and can work with any type T.
   - The method printValue() takes a parameter of type T and prints its value.

   Using the generic method:

```java
java

public class Main {
    public static void main(String[] args)
{
        Main obj = new Main();
        obj.printValue("Hello");        //
Output: Hello
        obj.printValue(123);            //
Output: 123
    }

    // Generic method
    public <T> void printValue(T value) {
        System.out.println(value);
    }
}
```

Here, the printValue() method is used with both a String and an Integer without any need for casting, making the method flexible and type-safe.

Wildcards and Bounded Types in Generics

Wildcards are a powerful feature in generics that allow you to use a type parameter without knowing its specific type. Wildcards are useful when you want to specify an unknown type but still maintain certain constraints on that type.

1. **Unbounded Wildcards**: An **unbounded wildcard** is represented by the ? symbol. It can represent any type.

   Example:

   ```java
   public void printList(List<?> list) {
       for (Object item : list) {
           System.out.println(item);
       }
   }
   ```

   In this example, the method `printList()` can accept a `List` of any type (`List<String>`, `List<Integer>`, etc.), but since the wildcard is unbounded, we can only access the elements as `Object` types.

2. **Bounded Wildcards**: A **bounded wildcard** allows you to restrict the types that can be used. There are two main types of bounded wildcards:
   - **Upper-bounded wildcard** (`? extends T`): Specifies that the type must be a subclass of `T` (including `T` itself).
   - **Lower-bounded wildcard** (`? super T`): Specifies that the type must be a superclass of `T` (including `T` itself).

Example of Upper-bounded Wildcard:

java

```java
public void printNumbers(List<? extends
Number> list) {
    for (Number num : list) {
        System.out.println(num);
    }
}
```

This method accepts a `List` of any class that extends `Number`, such as `Integer`, `Double`, or `Float`.

Example of Lower-bounded Wildcard:

java

```java
public void addIntegers(List<? super
Integer> list) {
    list.add(10);  // Adding Integer to the
list
}
```

This method accepts a `List` of any class that is a superclass of `Integer`, such as `Object` or `Number`.

Real-World Analogy: Generic Container for Different Types of Objects

To illustrate how generics work in a real-world scenario, let's imagine a **Generic Container** that can store different types of objects. This container can hold anything from strings, integers, or custom objects, while still maintaining type safety.

1. **Generic Container Class**:

```java
public class Container<T> {
    private T item;

    public void store(T item) {
        this.item = item;
    }

    public T retrieve() {
        return item;
    }
}
```

In this example, the `Container` class is generic and can store any type of object, such as `String`, `Integer`, or any other custom type.

2. **Using the Generic Container**:

```
java

public class Main {
    public static void main(String[] args)
{

        Container<String>  stringContainer
= new Container<>();
        stringContainer.store("Hello");

System.out.println(stringContainer.retrie
ve());  // Output: Hello

        Container<Integer>  intContainer  =
new Container<>();
        intContainer.store(123);

System.out.println(intContainer.retrieve(
));  // Output: 123
    }
}
```

In this example, we create two `Container` objects: one for storing `String` and one for storing `Integer`. The `store()` method accepts the object of the appropriate type, and the `retrieve()` method safely returns the object of the correct type without requiring casting.

Summary

In this chapter, we covered the following key aspects of **Generics in Java**:

- **What are Generics**: Generics allow you to write flexible and reusable code while ensuring type safety at compile time.
- **Creating and Using Generic Classes and Methods**: We saw how to define and use generic classes and methods to work with any data type while maintaining type safety.
- **Wildcards and Bounded Types**: We explored how wildcards (?) allow you to specify unknown types, and how bounded wildcards (extends and super) help you constrain those types.
- **Real-World Analogy**: We demonstrated the use of a generic container class to store and retrieve different types of objects in a safe and reusable way.

Generics are a powerful tool in Java that allows you to build flexible and reusable code, and understanding how to use them effectively will help you write more efficient and maintainable programs. In the next chapters, we will continue to explore advanced Java concepts, including collections, exception handling, and more.

CHAPTER 13

JAVA STREAMS AND LAMBDA EXPRESSIONS

Java Streams and Lambda Expressions provide a functional programming approach to working with collections and data in Java. They allow you to express operations on collections more concisely, improving both readability and maintainability. In this chapter, we will introduce the Java Streams API, explore functional programming concepts in Java, demonstrate how to use lambda expressions to process data, and look at a real-world example of filtering and mapping data from a list.

Introduction to Java Streams API

The **Streams API** in Java, introduced in Java 8, is a powerful feature that allows you to process sequences of elements (such as collections, arrays, or I/O channels) in a functional style. Streams represent a sequence of data elements that can be processed in parallel or sequentially, and they provide a way to perform complex operations on data in a declarative manner.

Key features of Java Streams:

- **Declarative**: You specify *what* you want to do with the data, not *how* it should be done.
- **Pipeline**: Stream operations are typically chained together in a pipeline, where each operation is performed on the data.
- **Lazy Evaluation**: Operations on streams are not executed until a terminal operation is invoked. This allows for optimization.
- **Support for parallel processing**: Streams can easily be processed in parallel to improve performance when dealing with large datasets.

Basic Stream Operations:

1. **Intermediate Operations**: Operations that transform a stream into another stream (e.g., `filter()`, `map()`).
2. **Terminal Operations**: Operations that produce a result or a side-effect (e.g., `collect()`, `forEach()`, `reduce()`).

Creating a Stream: A stream can be created from a collection, array, or other data sources.

Example:

```java

import java.util.List;
```

143

```java
import java.util.stream.Stream;

public class Main {
    public static void main(String[] args) {
        // Creating a Stream from a collection
        List<String> list = List.of("apple",
"banana", "cherry");
        Stream<String> stream = list.stream();

        // Perform operations on the stream
        stream.forEach(System.out::println);
    }
}
```

This example demonstrates creating a stream from a `List` and using the `forEach()` terminal operation to print each element.

Functional Programming Concepts in Java

Functional programming (FP) is a programming paradigm that treats computation as the evaluation of mathematical functions and avoids changing state or mutable data. Java, traditionally an object-oriented language, introduced functional programming features in Java 8, allowing you to take advantage of immutability, first-class functions, and lambda expressions.

Key concepts of functional programming in Java:

1. **First-Class Functions**: Functions can be treated as objects, passed around as parameters, and returned from other functions.

2. **Immutability**: Once an object is created, it cannot be changed. Streams in Java are immutable, meaning each operation on a stream produces a new stream.

3. **Higher-Order Functions**: Functions that take other functions as parameters or return functions. This is where lambda expressions shine.

Using Lambdas to Process Data

Lambda expressions were introduced in Java 8 as a way to implement functional interfaces (interfaces with just one abstract method) in a more concise and readable way. They provide a clear and expressive syntax to represent a method interface with an expression.

Syntax of a Lambda Expression:

```java

(parameters) -> expression
```

Example of a Lambda Expression:

```java
```

```java
// Traditional way to define a runnable
Runnable runnable1 = new Runnable() {
    public void run() {
        System.out.println("Hello, world!");
    }
};

// Using a lambda expression
Runnable        runnable2        =        ()        ->
System.out.println("Hello, world!");
runnable2.run();
```

Using Lambdas with Streams: Lambda expressions are commonly used with the Streams API to process data. They can be passed to methods like `map()`, `filter()`, and `forEach()` to transform and handle the data in a stream.

Example of using lambdas with Streams:

```java
java

import java.util.List;
import java.util.stream.Collectors;

public class Main {
    public static void main(String[] args) {
        List<String> fruits = List.of("apple",
"banana", "cherry", "date", "elderberry");
```

146

```
        // Using lambda expression to filter and
map
        List<String> result = fruits.stream()

.filter(fruit  ->  fruit.startsWith("b"))    //
Filter fruits starting with 'b'

.map(String::toUpperCase)        //   Convert   to
uppercase

.collect(Collectors.toList());   // Collect  the
result into a list

        result.forEach(System.out::println);
    }
}
```

Output:

```
nginx
```

```
BANANA
```

In this example:

- **filter()** is an intermediate operation that only allows elements starting with the letter "b" to pass through.

- **map()** is another intermediate operation that transforms the elements, converting them to uppercase.
- **collect()** is a terminal operation that collects the result into a list.

Real-World Example: Filtering and Mapping Data from a List

Let's say you have a list of student records, and you need to process the data to get the names of students who passed (those with a grade above 60), convert their names to uppercase, and sort the results.

1. **Student Class**:

   java

   ```java
   public class Student {
       private String name;
       private double grade;

       public Student(String name, double grade) {
           this.name = name;
           this.grade = grade;
       }

       public String getName() {
           return name;
   ```

```
        }

    public double getGrade() {
        return grade;
    }
}
```

2. **Processing the Data with Streams and Lambdas**:

```java
import java.util.List;
import java.util.stream.Collectors;

public class Main {
    public static void main(String[] args)
    {
        List<Student> students = List.of(
            new Student("Alice", 85),
            new Student("Bob", 58),
            new Student("Charlie", 72),
            new Student("David", 50)
        );

        // Using Streams and Lambdas to
filter, map, and collect data
        List<String> passingStudents =
students.stream()
```

149

```
.filter(student -> student.getGrade() >
60)  // Only students who passed

.map(student                             ->
student.getName().toUpperCase())         //
Convert names to uppercase

.sorted()  // Sort names alphabetically

.collect(Collectors.toList());  // Collect
into a list


passingStudents.forEach(System.out::print
ln);
    }
}
```

Output:

```
nginx

ALICE
CHARLIE
```

Explanation:

- o **filter()**: Filters the stream to include only students with grades above 60.

150

- o **map()**: Converts each student's name to uppercase.

- o **sorted()**: Sorts the names alphabetically.

- o **collect()**: Collects the final result into a list.

Summary

In this chapter, we have covered:

- **Java Streams API**: A powerful tool for working with sequences of data in a functional style, providing a way to perform operations on collections without modifying the underlying data.

- **Functional Programming Concepts**: We explored concepts such as first-class functions, immutability, and higher-order functions, which are key features of functional programming and are enabled in Java via Streams and Lambda expressions.

- **Lambda Expressions**: A concise way to represent methods, which are especially useful when working with the Streams API. They allow for more readable and expressive code.

- **Real-World Example**: We worked through a real-world example of filtering, mapping, and sorting student data, demonstrating how Streams and Lambdas can simplify complex data processing tasks.

Streams and Lambda expressions help you write cleaner, more readable, and maintainable code, especially when dealing with collections. By embracing functional programming in Java, you can leverage the full power of the Streams API to process data efficiently and effectively. In the next chapters, we will continue to explore other advanced features of Java that will help you develop more robust and flexible applications.

CHAPTER 14

WORKING WITH FILES AND I/O IN JAVA

Handling files and input/output (I/O) is a common task in programming. Java provides a robust set of I/O classes that allow you to work with files, directories, and streams. In this chapter, we will explore Java I/O basics, focusing on file handling, reading from and writing to files, working with directories and file paths, and a real-world application involving log file reading and processing.

Java I/O Basics (File Handling, FileReader, FileWriter)

Java's **I/O API** provides a set of classes and methods for reading from and writing to files, among other I/O operations. Two commonly used classes for file reading and writing are `FileReader` and `FileWriter`. They allow you to handle text-based file I/O.

1. **FileReader**: A class used to read data from a file character by character. It's suitable for reading text files.
2. **FileWriter**: A class used to write data to a file character by character. It's used to write text data to a file.

153

Here's a basic example demonstrating how to use `FileReader` and `FileWriter`:

java

```java
import java.io.FileReader;
import java.io.FileWriter;
import java.io.IOException;

public class FileExample {
    public static void main(String[] args) {
        // Writing to a file using FileWriter
        try (FileWriter writer = new FileWriter("example.txt")) {
            writer.write("Hello, this is a test file!");
        } catch (IOException e) {
            System.out.println("Error writing to the file: " + e.getMessage());
        }

        // Reading from a file using FileReader
        try (FileReader reader = new FileReader("example.txt")) {
            int character;
            while ((character = reader.read()) != -1) {
                System.out.print((char) character); // Output the content of the file
```

```
        }
    } catch (IOException e) {
        System.out.println("Error    reading
the file: " + e.getMessage());
    }
  }
}
```

Explanation:

- **Writing to a file**: The `FileWriter` class is used to write a string to a file named `example.txt`. If the file doesn't exist, it is created.

- **Reading from a file**: The `FileReader` class is used to read the contents of `example.txt`. The `read()` method reads one character at a time.

Note: The `try-with-resources` statement ensures that both the `FileWriter` and `FileReader` resources are automatically closed after use, even if an exception occurs.

Reading from and Writing to Files

1. **Reading from a File**: To read from a file, you can use classes like `FileReader`, `BufferedReader`, or `Scanner`. These classes help read text data efficiently.

   o **Using BufferedReader for efficient reading**:

```java
java

import java.io.BufferedReader;
import java.io.FileReader;
import java.io.IOException;

public class FileReaderExample {
    public static void main(String[] args) {
        try (BufferedReader reader = new BufferedReader(new FileReader("example.txt"))) {
            String line;
            while ((line = reader.readLine()) != null) {
                System.out.println(line); // Output each line of the file
            }
        } catch (IOException e) {
            System.out.println("Error reading the file: " + e.getMessage());
        }
    }
}
```

Explanation:

- o The `BufferedReader` class is more efficient than `FileReader` when reading large files because it reads data in larger chunks.

2. **Writing to a File**: To write data to a file, you can use classes like `FileWriter` or `BufferedWriter`. These classes allow you to write text data to files.

    - o **Using BufferedWriter for efficient writing**:

```java
import java.io.BufferedWriter;
import java.io.FileWriter;
import java.io.IOException;

public class FileWriterExample {
    public static void main(String[] args) {
        try (BufferedWriter writer = new
BufferedWriter(new
FileWriter("output.txt"))) {
            writer.write("This is a test
message.");
            writer.newLine();  // Adds a
new line
            writer.write("This is another
line.");
        } catch (IOException e) {
            System.out.println("Error
writing to the file: " + e.getMessage());
```

157

```
            }
         }
      }
```

Explanation:

- o The `BufferedWriter` class is used here for efficient writing to the `output.txt` file. It writes characters in bulk to optimize the process, which is especially useful when writing large files.

Handling Directories and File Paths

In addition to reading and writing files, Java provides classes for working with directories and file paths. The `File` class can be used to manipulate files and directories.

1. **Creating Directories**:

```java

import java.io.File;
import java.io.IOException;

public class DirectoryExample {
    public static void main(String[] args)
{
```

```java
        File     directory     =     new
File("testDirectory");

        // Create a new directory
        if (!directory.exists()) {
            if (directory.mkdir()) {

System.out.println("Directory     created
successfully.");
            } else {

System.out.println("Failed  to  create  the
directory.");
            }
        } else {
            System.out.println("Directory
already exists.");
        }
    }
}
```

2. **Listing Files in a Directory**:

```java
java

import java.io.File;

public class ListFilesExample {
    public static void main(String[] args)
{
```

```
        File       directory      =       new
File("testDirectory");
        String[]          fileList         =
directory.list();

        if (fileList != null) {
            for    (String    fileName    :
fileList) {

System.out.println(fileName);
                }
        } else {
            System.out.println("The
directory is empty or does not exist.");
            }
        }
}
```

3. **File Paths**:

   o Use the `getAbsolutePath()` method to get the
      absolute path of a file or directory:

```
java
```

```
File file = new File("example.txt");
System.out.println("Absolute    Path:    "    +
file.getAbsolutePath());
```

o You can use `Paths` and `Files` classes (introduced in Java 7) for better handling of file paths and directories.

Real-World Application: Log File Reading and Processing

In many applications, you need to read and process log files to monitor activity or troubleshoot issues. Java makes it easy to work with log files by reading them line by line and processing the contents. Here's an example that demonstrates how to read a log file, filter out error messages, and print them.

1. **Log File Example** (log.txt):

```
pgsql
```

```
INFO: Application started
ERROR: Null pointer exception at line 45
INFO: User logged in
ERROR: Database connection failed
DEBUG: Debugging user authentication
```

2. **Reading and Processing the Log File**:

```
java
```

```
import java.io.BufferedReader;
import java.io.FileReader;
```

161

```java
import java.io.IOException;

public class LogFileProcessor {
    public static void main(String[] args)
{

        String logFilePath = "log.txt";

        try (BufferedReader reader = new
BufferedReader(new
FileReader(logFilePath))) {
            String line;
            while          ((line         =
reader.readLine()) != null) {
                if
(line.startsWith("ERROR")) {

System.out.println("Error Log: " + line);
                }
            }
        } catch (IOException e) {
            System.out.println("Error
reading the log file: " + e.getMessage());
        }
    }
}
```

Explanation:

- o The `BufferedReader` is used to read the log file line by line.
- o The program filters out only the lines that start with "ERROR" and prints them, which can be useful for debugging or error tracking.

Output:

```pgsql
Error Log: ERROR: Null pointer exception at line
45
Error Log: ERROR: Database connection failed
```

Summary

In this chapter, we have covered:

- **Java I/O Basics**: We explored the basic classes and methods (`FileReader`, `FileWriter`, `BufferedReader`, `BufferedWriter`) used for reading from and writing to files in Java.
- **Handling Directories and File Paths**: We learned how to create directories, list files, and manipulate file paths using the `File` class.

163

- **Real-World Application**: We walked through an example of reading and processing a log file, filtering error messages and printing them to the console.

Understanding how to work with files and directories is essential for developing Java applications that need to process data stored in external files. The tools provided by Java's I/O API allow you to perform file operations efficiently, handle errors, and manage resources effectively. In the next chapters, we will continue to explore more advanced features and best practices in Java programming.

CHAPTER 15

JAVA MEMORY MANAGEMENT AND GARBAGE COLLECTION

Memory management is a crucial aspect of Java programming. Java's memory management system allows developers to work with large-scale applications efficiently while minimizing the risk of memory-related errors like memory leaks. This chapter explores how Java handles memory management, the concept of **garbage collection**, and how you can optimize memory usage. We will also discuss memory leaks and provide a real-world example of resource management in server applications.

How Java Handles Memory Management

Java's memory management system is largely automated and designed to relieve developers from managing memory manually, as is required in languages like C or C++. Java's memory management involves the following key concepts:

1. **Heap Memory**:
   o The **heap** is the area of memory where Java objects are dynamically allocated.

165

- o When you create an object using the `new` keyword, Java allocates memory for that object in the heap.
- o The heap is divided into two regions: the **young generation** and the **old generation** (also called the **tenured generation**).

2. **Stack Memory**:
   - o The **stack** is used for storing local variables and method calls. It follows a last-in, first-out (LIFO) order.
   - o Each thread in a Java application has its own stack, which helps in managing method calls and local variables.
   - o Unlike the heap, memory in the stack is automatically managed as methods are called and variables go out of scope.

3. **Method Area**:
   - o The **method area** is used for storing class structures, method metadata, and constants.
   - o It is shared among all threads in a Java application and contains data that doesn't change frequently.

Java's memory management works by allocating memory to objects in the heap, where the memory for an object is reclaimed when it is no longer in use. The system automatically manages memory, freeing up resources through **garbage collection**.

What is Garbage Collection and How Does It Work?

Garbage Collection (GC) in Java is a process of automatically reclaiming memory that is no longer in use by the program. It is responsible for identifying and removing objects that are no longer referenced, freeing up memory for new objects. This helps in preventing memory leaks, which can occur when objects are left in memory but are no longer needed.

1. **How Garbage Collection Works**:
    o **Mark and Sweep**: The garbage collector works in phases. First, it marks objects that are still reachable or in use, and then it sweeps or removes objects that are no longer referenced.
    o **Generational Garbage Collection**: Java uses a generational garbage collection strategy, which divides the heap into generations to optimize performance. The idea is that younger objects (those created recently) are more likely to become unreachable quickly, so they are collected more frequently.
        ▪ **Young Generation**: Contains objects that are recently created. Most objects in this area are short-lived and can be collected quickly.

167

- **Old Generation**: Contains objects that have survived several garbage collection cycles and are expected to live longer.
- **Permanent Generation** (in older versions of Java): Contains metadata about classes and methods.

2. **Phases of Garbage Collection**:

o **Minor GC**: Occurs when the **young generation** fills up. It is a fast process since only a small portion of memory is involved.

o **Major GC**: Occurs when the **old generation** fills up. This is more time-consuming because it involves collecting more objects.

o **Full GC**: A full garbage collection occurs when both the young and old generations need to be collected. It is a comprehensive and expensive process.

2. **Garbage Collection Algorithms**:

o **Serial Garbage Collector**: A simple collector designed for single-threaded environments.

o **Parallel Garbage Collector**: Uses multiple threads for garbage collection, improving throughput for multi-threaded applications.

- o **Concurrent Mark-Sweep (CMS) Garbage Collector**: A low-latency collector that minimizes the time spent on garbage collection.
- o **G1 Garbage Collector**: A modern collector that aims to provide low-latency while managing large heaps.

Analyzing Memory Leaks and Optimization

While Java's garbage collector automatically frees memory, memory leaks can still occur if objects are unintentionally held in memory, preventing garbage collection from reclaiming their space.

Memory Leaks in Java: A **memory leak** occurs when objects that are no longer needed remain referenced and therefore cannot be garbage collected. This typically happens when:

- Objects are stored in collections or caches and are not removed after use.
- Circular references exist, preventing garbage collection from detecting unused objects.

Signs of Memory Leaks:

- Increased memory usage over time with no significant release of memory.

169

- OutOfMemoryError exceptions when the heap space is exhausted.

Tools to Detect Memory Leaks:

1. **JVM Profilers**: Tools like **JVisualVM** and **JProfiler** help analyze memory usage and detect objects that are not being garbage collected.
2. **Heap Dumps**: A heap dump can be analyzed to find memory leaks. Tools like **Eclipse MAT** (Memory Analyzer Tool) allow you to examine heap dumps and identify memory leaks.

Optimizing Garbage Collection:

1. **Minimize Object Creation**: Frequent creation of short-lived objects can lead to high garbage collection activity. Reuse objects when possible.
2. **Manage Large Objects**: Large objects that are rarely used should be moved to the **old generation** to reduce the frequency of garbage collection.
3. **Use Weak References**: If you want an object to be garbage collected when memory is low, use **WeakReference** or **SoftReference**.
4. **Tune JVM Garbage Collection Settings**: You can tune garbage collection settings based on the application's needs, such as adjusting the heap size or selecting a

specific garbage collector algorithm (e.g., –XX:+UseG1GC for G1).

Real-World Example: Resource Management in Server Applications

In server applications, resource management is critical for maintaining performance and avoiding resource leaks. For example, a web server that manages multiple client connections needs to ensure that resources like network connections, threads, and memory are properly managed to prevent performance degradation or crashes.

Example: Connection Pool Management in a Web Server: Imagine a web server that handles database connections. Each client request requires access to the database, but opening and closing database connections for each request can be inefficient. Instead, the server uses a **connection pool** to reuse database connections. However, it is important to manage the connections properly to avoid memory leaks.

1. **Simulating Connection Pool**:

```java
java

public class ConnectionPool {
```

171

```java
    private         List<DatabaseConnection>
availableConnections;
    private         List<DatabaseConnection>
inUseConnections;

    public ConnectionPool(int size) {
        availableConnections    =    new
ArrayList<>();
        inUseConnections        =    new
ArrayList<>();
        // Initialize the pool with
connections
        for (int i = 0; i < size; i++) {
            availableConnections.add(new
DatabaseConnection());
        }
    }

    // Borrow a connection from the pool
    public              DatabaseConnection
borrowConnection() {
        if
(availableConnections.isEmpty()) {
            throw new RuntimeException("No
available connections.");
        }
        DatabaseConnection connection  =
availableConnections.remove(0);
        inUseConnections.add(connection);
```

```java
        return connection;
    }

    // Return a connection to the pool
    public                         void
returnConnection(DatabaseConnection
connection) {

inUseConnections.remove(connection);

availableConnections.add(connection);
    }

    public void closeAllConnections() {
        // Close all in-use and available
connections

availableConnections.forEach(DatabaseConn
ection::close);

inUseConnections.forEach(DatabaseConnecti
on::close);
    }
}

class DatabaseConnection {
    public void close() {
        // Simulate closing the connection
```

173

```
        System.out.println("Closing
database connection.");
    }
}
```

2. **Managing Connections and Avoiding Leaks**:

   o The **ConnectionPool** class manages a fixed number of database connections.

   o The **borrowConnection()** method retrieves an available connection and marks it as in use.

   o The **returnConnection()** method returns the connection to the pool after use.

   o The **closeAllConnections()** method ensures that all connections are properly closed when the server shuts down, preventing resource leaks.

3. **Usage Example**:

```java
public class Main {
    public static void main(String[] args)
{
        ConnectionPool    pool    =    new
ConnectionPool(5); // Create a pool with 5
connections

        // Borrow and return connections
```

```
        DatabaseConnection    connection1    =
pool.borrowConnection();

pool.returnConnection(connection1);

        DatabaseConnection    connection2    =
pool.borrowConnection();

pool.returnConnection(connection2);

        // Close all connections when done
        pool.closeAllConnections();
    }
}
```

Output:

```
pgsql

Closing database connection.
Closing database connection.
Closing database connection.
Closing database connection.
Closing database connection.
```

Explanation:

- The connection pool ensures that database connections are reused efficiently.

175

- The `closeAllConnections()` method ensures that all database connections are properly closed when no longer needed, preventing memory leaks and resource exhaustion.
- If connections are not properly returned or closed, it could result in **resource leaks**, where the connections remain in memory, consuming resources even though they are no longer in use.

Summary

In this chapter, we covered:

- **Java Memory Management**: Java's memory management system includes heap, stack, and method area memory. The heap is where objects are allocated and managed by the garbage collector.
- **Garbage Collection**: We discussed how Java's garbage collection automatically reclaims memory that is no longer in use by identifying and removing unreachable objects.
- **Memory Leaks and Optimization**: We explored how memory leaks occur, how to detect them, and how to optimize garbage collection and memory usage in Java applications.

- **Real-World Example**: We provided a real-world example of managing database connections in a connection pool, demonstrating how to handle resources efficiently in server applications to avoid memory leaks.

Memory management and garbage collection play a crucial role in the performance and stability of Java applications, especially in large-scale systems. By understanding and optimizing memory management, you can ensure that your Java applications run efficiently without running into memory-related issues.

CHAPTER 16

JAVA THREADS AND CONCURRENCY

In modern software development, **concurrency** is a critical concept, especially for building efficient applications that can handle multiple tasks simultaneously. **Threads** are the fundamental units of execution within a Java program. This chapter will introduce you to Java threads, explain why concurrency is important, how to create and manage threads, and how to ensure thread safety with synchronization. We will also look at a real-world example of a multi-threaded download manager to see how concurrency is applied.

What Are Threads and Why Is Concurrency Important?

A **thread** is a lightweight sub-process or unit of execution within a process. Each thread represents a single path of execution and operates independently of other threads within the same process. A process can have multiple threads running in parallel, and each thread shares the same memory space, which makes threads more efficient for certain tasks compared to processes that run in separate memory spaces.

Concurrency refers to the ability of a program to perform multiple tasks at the same time, or in overlapping periods. This is particularly important for modern applications, where resources like CPU cores, memory, and I/O operations can be utilized more effectively. By running tasks concurrently, programs can improve performance and responsiveness.

Why is concurrency important?

- **Efficiency**: It allows tasks to run in parallel, fully utilizing available CPU cores, which is crucial for performance in multi-core systems.
- **Responsiveness**: In GUI applications or web servers, concurrent execution ensures that one task doesn't block others, providing a more responsive user experience.
- **Asynchronous Operations**: Concurrency allows for asynchronous operations, like reading from a file or fetching data from the web, which can continue running in the background while other tasks are processed.

However, concurrency also introduces complexities, such as the potential for **race conditions** and **data corruption**, which requires careful management of threads to ensure thread safety.

Creating and Managing Threads

In Java, threads are represented by the Thread class and can be created in two primary ways: by extending the Thread class or by implementing the Runnable interface.

1. **Creating Threads by Extending the Thread Class**: You can create a custom thread by extending the Thread class and overriding the run() method, which defines the code to be executed by the thread.

   Example:

   java

```java
public class MyThread extends Thread {
    @Override
    public void run() {
        System.out.println("Thread        is
running...");
    }

    public static void main(String[] args)
{
        MyThread thread = new MyThread();
        thread.start();    // Starts the
thread
    }
}
```

Explanation:

- o We create a class `MyThread` that extends the `Thread` class and overrides the `run()` method.
- o The `start()` method is called to begin the execution of the thread, which internally calls the `run()` method.

2. **Creating Threads by Implementing the `Runnable` Interface**: Another way to create a thread is by implementing the `Runnable` interface, which is often preferred as it allows your class to extend another class (since Java does not support multiple inheritance).

Example:

```java
public class MyRunnable implements Runnable {
    @Override
    public void run() {
        System.out.println("Runnable thread is running...");
    }

    public static void main(String[] args) {
```

```
        MyRunnable     task    =     new
MyRunnable();
        Thread thread = new Thread(task);
        thread.start();    // Starts   the
thread
    }
}
```

Explanation:

- The `MyRunnable` class implements the `Runnable` interface and provides an implementation of the `run()` method.
- We create a new `Thread` object and pass the `Runnable` instance to its constructor. Then, we call the `start()` method to initiate the thread.

3. **Managing Threads**:
   - **Thread States**: A thread can be in one of several states: **New, Runnable, Blocked, Waiting, Timed Waiting**, and **Terminated**.
   - **Thread Priorities**: Java allows you to set thread priorities using the `setPriority()` method, influencing the order in which threads are scheduled.
   - **Thread Joining**: The `join()` method allows one thread to wait for another thread to finish execution.

Example:

```java

public class ThreadExample {
    public static void main(String[] args)
throws InterruptedException {
        Thread thread1 = new Thread(() ->
{
            System.out.println("Thread   1
is running...");
        });

        Thread thread2 = new Thread(() ->
{
            System.out.println("Thread   2
is running...");
        });

        thread1.start();
        thread2.start();

        thread1.join();     // Waits   for
thread1 to finish
        thread2.join();     // Waits   for
thread2 to finish

        System.out.println("Both   threads
are finished.");
    }
```

```
}
```

Explanation:

o   We create and start two threads (`thread1` and `thread2`).

o   The `join()` method ensures that the main thread waits for both threads to finish before printing the final message.

Synchronization and Thread Safety

In a multi-threaded environment, multiple threads may try to access and modify shared resources simultaneously, leading to **race conditions** and data inconsistency. **Synchronization** is used to control access to shared resources and ensure that only one thread can access a critical section of code at a time.

1. **Synchronized Methods**: You can synchronize methods to prevent concurrent access to them. This ensures that only one thread can execute the method at any given time.

   Example:

   ```java
   public class Counter {
   ```

```java
    private int count = 0;

    // Synchronized method to ensure
thread-safe increment
    public synchronized void increment() {
        count++;
    }

    public int getCount() {
        return count;
    }
}
```

Explanation:

- o The `increment()` method is synchronized, ensuring that only one thread can increment the counter at a time.
- o This prevents race conditions when multiple threads call `increment()` simultaneously.

2. **Synchronized Blocks**: If you need to synchronize only a part of a method, you can use synchronized blocks.

Example:

```java
java

public class Counter {
    private int count = 0;
```

```
public void increment() {
        synchronized   (this)    {        //
Synchronized block
             count++;
        }
    }

    public int getCount() {
        return count;
    }
}
```

Explanation:

o The synchronized block ensures that only one thread can execute the code inside the block at a time, thus avoiding race conditions.

Real-World Example: Multi-Threaded Download Manager

Let's consider a real-world application where multiple files are being downloaded concurrently in a multi-threaded download manager. Each download operation will run in a separate thread, and we'll ensure that resources like memory and network connections are handled correctly.

1. **DownloadTask Class**: This class will simulate the process of downloading a file.

```java
public class DownloadTask implements
Runnable {
    private String fileName;

    public DownloadTask(String fileName) {
        this.fileName = fileName;
    }

    @Override
    public void run() {
        System.out.println("Downloading  "
+ fileName + "...");
        try {
            Thread.sleep(2000);          //
Simulate time taken to download
            System.out.println(fileName +
" downloaded successfully.");
        } catch (InterruptedException e) {
            System.out.println("Download
interrupted: " + fileName);
        }
    }
}
```

2. **DownloadManager Class**: This class manages the downloading of multiple files.

java

```java
public class DownloadManager {
    public void startDownloads(List<String> files) {
        List<Thread> threads = new ArrayList<>();
        for (String file : files) {
            DownloadTask task = new DownloadTask(file);
            Thread thread = new Thread(task);
            thread.start();
            threads.add(thread);
        }

        // Wait for all threads to finish
        for (Thread thread : threads) {
            try {
                thread.join();
            } catch (InterruptedException e) {
                e.printStackTrace();
            }
        }
```

```
        System.out.println("All   downloads
completed.");
    }
}
```

3. **Using the DownloadManager**:

```
java

public class Main {
    public static void main(String[] args)
{
        List<String>   filesToDownload   =
List.of("File1.txt",        "File2.txt",
"File3.txt");
        DownloadManager   manager   =   new
DownloadManager();

manager.startDownloads(filesToDownload);
    }
}
```

Explanation:

o   The `DownloadTask` class simulates
   downloading a file by sleeping for 2 seconds and
   printing messages.

189

o   The `DownloadManager` class manages multiple download tasks, creating a new thread for each file.

o   The `join()` method ensures that the main thread waits for all download threads to complete before printing the final message.

Output:

css

```
Downloading File1.txt...
Downloading File2.txt...
Downloading File3.txt...
File1.txt downloaded successfully.
File2.txt downloaded successfully.
File3.txt downloaded successfully.
All downloads completed.
```

Explanation:

- Each file is downloaded concurrently in a separate thread, allowing multiple downloads to occur at the same time.

- The `join()` method ensures that the main thread waits for all downloads to finish before printing the "All downloads completed." message.

190

Summary

In this chapter, we have covered the following key concepts related to **Java Threads and Concurrency**:

- **Threads**: Threads are individual units of execution within a process, enabling concurrent tasks in a program.
- **Concurrency**: Concurrency is crucial for improving performance and responsiveness in applications by running multiple tasks simultaneously.
- **Creating and Managing Threads**: Threads can be created using the `Thread` class or by implementing the `Runnable` interface. We explored how to manage and control threads, including starting, joining, and managing their state.
- **Synchronization**: Synchronization ensures that only one thread can access a resource at a time, preventing race conditions and ensuring thread safety.
- **Real-World Example**: We created a multi-threaded download manager to simulate downloading files concurrently using Java threads.

Understanding threads and concurrency is essential for building efficient, responsive, and scalable applications. By using Java's threading and synchronization features, you can develop programs that leverage the full power of modern multi-core processors.

CHAPTER 17

WORKING WITH DATABASES IN JAVA

Database interaction is a crucial part of most applications, as they often need to store and retrieve persistent data. Java provides a standard API called **JDBC (Java Database Connectivity)** for connecting to databases, executing SQL queries, and processing results. In this chapter, we will explore the basics of JDBC, how to connect to a database, execute queries, handle SQL exceptions, and manage transactions. We will also implement a real-world example demonstrating CRUD (Create, Read, Update, Delete) operations on an **Employee** database.

JDBC (Java Database Connectivity) Basics

JDBC (Java Database Connectivity) is a Java API that enables Java applications to interact with relational databases. It provides methods for connecting to a database, executing SQL queries, and processing results.

Key Components of JDBC:

1. **DriverManager**: Manages a list of database drivers and establishes database connections.

2. **Connection**: Represents a connection to a specific database.

3. **Statement**: Used to execute SQL queries.

4. **ResultSet**: Contains the data retrieved by a SELECT query.

5. **SQLException**: Handles errors related to database access.

The typical workflow for using JDBC involves:

- **Establishing a connection** to the database.
- **Creating a statement** to execute SQL queries.
- **Executing queries** (such as SELECT, INSERT, UPDATE, or DELETE).
- **Handling the results**.
- **Closing the connection** to the database.

Connecting to a Database and Executing Queries

1. **Setting Up the Database**: To begin, you need a database to interact with. Let's assume we are using MySQL, but JDBC works with other databases like PostgreSQL, SQLite, or Oracle as well. You'll also need the appropriate JDBC driver for the database you are using.

Example for MySQL:

- o Download the MySQL JDBC driver (e.g., `mysql-connector-java.jar`).
- o Add it to the project's classpath.

2. **Establishing a Connection**: To connect to the database, you use the `DriverManager.getConnection()` method, providing the connection URL, database username, and password.

Syntax:

```java
Connection connection = DriverManager.getConnection("jdbc:mysql://localhost:3306/database_name", "username", "password");
```

3. **Executing Queries**:
   - o **Creating a statement**:

```java
Statement stmt = connection.createStatement();
```

   - o **Executing an INSERT query**:

```java
```

```java
String sql = "INSERT INTO employees
(name, position, salary) VALUES
('John Doe', 'Developer', 80000)";
stmt.executeUpdate(sql);
```

o **Executing a SELECT query**:

```java
```

```java
String sql = "SELECT * FROM
employees";
ResultSet rs =
stmt.executeQuery(sql);
```

4. **Example of connecting to a MySQL database**:
5. java
6.
7. import java.sql.*;
8.
9. public class JDBCExample {
10.   public static void main(String[]
   args) {
11.   try {
12.   // Load and register MySQL
   driver
13.
   Class.forName("com.mysql.cj.jdbc.Driver")
   ;
```
```

```
14.
15.              // Establish connection to
    the database
16.              Connection   connection   =
    DriverManager.getConnection(
17.
    "jdbc:mysql://localhost:3306/company_db",
    "root", "password");
18.
19.              // Create a statement object
20.              Statement   statement   =
    connection.createStatement();
21.
22.              // Execute an INSERT query
23.              String insertQuery = "INSERT
    INTO  employees  (name,  position,  salary)
    VALUES ('John Doe', 'Developer', 80000)";
24.
    statement.executeUpdate(insertQuery);
25.              System.out.println("Employee
    added successfully.");
26.
27.              // Execute a SELECT query
28.              String selectQuery = "SELECT
    * FROM employees";
29.              ResultSet   resultSet   =
    statement.executeQuery(selectQuery);
30.
31.              // Process the result set
```

```
32.            while (resultSet.next()) {
33.                int           id        =
   resultSet.getInt("id");
34.                String        name      =
   resultSet.getString("name");
35.                String     position     =
   resultSet.getString("position");
36.                double      salary       =
   resultSet.getDouble("salary");
37.                System.out.println("ID:
   " + id + ", Name: " + name + ", Position:
   " + position + ", Salary: " + salary);
38.            }
39.
40.            // Close the connection
41.            resultSet.close();
42.            statement.close();
43.            connection.close();
44.        }   catch    (SQLException    |
   ClassNotFoundException e) {
45.            e.printStackTrace();
46.        }
47.    }
48. }
```

49. **Explanation**:

  o We load the MySQL JDBC driver
  (Class.forName()), establish a connection
  using DriverManager.getConnection(),
  and create a Statement object.

- o We execute both an INSERT query and a SELECT query.
- o The ResultSet object stores the results of the SELECT query, and we process it using a loop.

Handling SQL Exceptions and Transactions

1. **SQL Exceptions**: SQLException is thrown when a database error occurs, such as invalid SQL syntax or connection issues. It provides detailed information about the error, including the error code and message.

   Handling SQL Exceptions:

   ```java
   java

   try {
       // Database operations
   } catch (SQLException e) {
       System.out.println("Error:      "     +
   e.getMessage());
       e.printStackTrace();
   }
   ```

2. **Transactions**: Java provides the ability to manage database transactions. By default, every SQL statement is

executed as a transaction. You can control transaction behavior by using the `setAutoCommit()` method.

Managing Transactions:

- o **Disabling Auto-Commit**: In most cases, you disable auto-commit mode to execute multiple queries as a single transaction.

```java
connection.setAutoCommit(false);
```

- o **Committing a Transaction**: Once all the queries in a transaction are executed successfully, you can commit the transaction to make the changes permanent.

```java
connection.commit();
```

- o **Rolling Back a Transaction**: If any query fails, you can roll back the entire transaction to undo all changes made during that transaction.

```java
connection.rollback();
```

Example of using transactions:

java

```
try {
    connection.setAutoCommit(false);    // Disable auto-commit

    // Execute some queries
    String updateSalary = "UPDATE employees SET salary = 90000 WHERE name = 'John Doe'";

    statement.executeUpdate(updateSalary);

    String insertNewEmployee = "INSERT INTO employees (name, position, salary) VALUES ('Jane Smith', 'Manager', 95000)";

    statement.executeUpdate(insertNewEmployee);

    // Commit the transaction
    connection.commit();
    System.out.println("Transaction completed successfully.");

} catch (SQLException e) {
    // Rollback the transaction if an error occurs
```

200

```
    try {
        connection.rollback();
        System.out.println("Transaction
rolled back due to error.");
    } catch (SQLException ex) {
        ex.printStackTrace();
    }
} finally {
    // Restore auto-commit mode
    try {
        connection.setAutoCommit(true);
    } catch (SQLException e) {
        e.printStackTrace();
    }
}
```

Real-World Example: Employee Database CRUD Operations

Now let's implement **CRUD (Create, Read, Update, Delete)** operations on an **Employee** database.

1. **Employee Table**: Assume we have an `employees` table with columns: `id`, `name`, `position`, and `salary`.

SQL Schema:

sql

```
CREATE TABLE employees (
```

```
        id INT AUTO_INCREMENT PRIMARY KEY,
        name VARCHAR(100),
        position VARCHAR(100),
        salary DOUBLE
);
```

2. **Employee Database Operations**:

Create (Insert a new employee):

java

```
public void createEmployee(Connection
connection, String name, String position,
double salary) throws SQLException {
    String sql = "INSERT INTO employees
(name, position, salary) VALUES (?, ?, ?)";
    try (PreparedStatement statement =
connection.prepareStatement(sql)) {
        statement.setString(1, name);
        statement.setString(2, position);
        statement.setDouble(3, salary);
        statement.executeUpdate();
    }
}
```

Read (Get employee details):

java

```java
public void getEmployeeById(Connection
connection, int id) throws SQLException {
    String sql = "SELECT * FROM employees
WHERE id = ?";
    try (PreparedStatement statement =
connection.prepareStatement(sql)) {
        statement.setInt(1, id);
        ResultSet rs =
statement.executeQuery();
        if (rs.next()) {
            System.out.println("ID: " +
rs.getInt("id"));
            System.out.println("Name: " +
rs.getString("name"));
            System.out.println("Position:
" + rs.getString("position"));
            System.out.println("Salary: "
+ rs.getDouble("salary"));
        }
    }
}
```

Update (Update employee salary):

```java
java
```

```java
public void
updateEmployeeSalary(Connection
connection, int id, double newSalary)
throws SQLException {
```

203

```java
    String sql = "UPDATE employees SET
salary = ? WHERE id = ?";
    try (PreparedStatement statement =
connection.prepareStatement(sql)) {
        statement.setDouble(1, newSalary);
        statement.setInt(2, id);
        statement.executeUpdate();
    }
}
```

Delete (Delete an employee):

java

```java
public void deleteEmployeeById(Connection
connection, int id) throws SQLException {
    String sql = "DELETE FROM employees
WHERE id = ?";
    try (PreparedStatement statement =
connection.prepareStatement(sql)) {
        statement.setInt(1, id);
        statement.executeUpdate();
    }
}
```

3. **Using the CRUD Methods**:

java

```java
public static void main(String[] args) {
```

```
try     (Connection     connection     =
DriverManager.getConnection("jdbc:mysql:/
/localhost:3306/company_db",          "root",
"password")) {
        // Create Employee
        createEmployee(connection,     "John
Doe", "Developer", 80000);

        // Read Employee
        getEmployeeById(connection, 1);

        // Update Employee Salary
        updateEmployeeSalary(connection,
1, 85000);

        // Delete Employee
        deleteEmployeeById(connection, 1);
    } catch (SQLException e) {
        e.printStackTrace();
    }
}
```

Explanation:

- The CRUD methods allow you to create, read, update, and delete employee records from the database using `PreparedStatement` for SQL queries.
- The `Connection` object is used to connect to the database, and exceptions are handled appropriately.

Summary

In this chapter, we have covered:

- **JDBC Basics**: Introduction to Java Database Connectivity (JDBC) and how to use it to connect to a database and execute SQL queries.
- **SQL Exceptions and Transactions**: How to handle exceptions in JDBC and manage transactions to ensure data consistency.
- **Real-World Example**: Implemented CRUD operations on an Employee database, demonstrating how to create, read, update, and delete records using JDBC.

Understanding how to interact with databases in Java is essential for building data-driven applications. JDBC provides a flexible way to work with relational databases, and mastering it will help you develop robust and scalable applications. In the next chapters, we will continue exploring advanced Java topics and techniques.

CHAPTER 18

JAVA NETWORKING

Java networking allows applications to communicate over a network, enabling them to exchange data with other systems or devices. Java provides a rich set of libraries for both **sockets** and **HTTP communication**, making it easy to build client-server applications, interact with APIs, and create web services. In this chapter, we will explore the fundamentals of Java networking, including sockets, HTTP, and working with APIs. We will also walk through a real-world example of building a simple chat application.

Introduction to Java Networking (Sockets, HTTP)

Java provides several classes in the `java.net` package to handle networking operations. The two main approaches for network communication are **sockets** and **HTTP**.

1. **Sockets**:

    o A **socket** is an endpoint for communication between two machines over a network.

207

- o Java provides the `Socket` class for client-side communication and the `ServerSocket` class for server-side communication.
- o Sockets use TCP (Transmission Control Protocol) or UDP (User Datagram Protocol) to establish reliable communication between clients and servers.

Basic Components of Sockets:

- o **Client**: A program that initiates a connection to a server.
- o **Server**: A program that listens for incoming connections from clients and processes their requests.

2. **HTTP**:
- o The **HTTP** protocol is used for web-based communication. Java provides libraries like `HttpURLConnection` and `HttpClient` (from Java 11) to make HTTP requests.
- o HTTP is stateless and follows a request-response model where the client sends an HTTP request, and the server responds with an HTTP response.

Java Networking Components:

- `Socket`: Used for creating a client that communicates with a server.
- `ServerSocket`: Used for creating a server that listens for incoming connections.
- `HttpURLConnection`: Used for making HTTP requests in Java (for example, to interact with RESTful APIs).

Creating a Simple Client-Server Application

Let's start by creating a simple client-server application using **sockets**. The server will listen for client connections, and the client will send a message to the server.

1. **Server-Side Code** (`Server.java`): The server listens on a specific port and accepts incoming client connections. It then reads the message sent by the client.

```java
java

import java.io.*;
import java.net.*;

public class Server {
    public static void main(String[] args)
{
        try {
```

```java
        // Create a ServerSocket that
listens on port 12345
        ServerSocket serverSocket =
new ServerSocket(12345);
        System.out.println("Server is
waiting for a connection...");

        // Accept incoming client
connection
        Socket clientSocket =
serverSocket.accept();
        System.out.println("Client
connected.");

        // Create input stream to read
data from the client
        BufferedReader reader = new
BufferedReader(new
InputStreamReader(clientSocket.getInputSt
ream()));
        String message =
reader.readLine();  // Read the message
from the client

        System.out.println("Received
from client: " + message);

        // Close the connection
        reader.close();
```

```
        clientSocket.close();
        serverSocket.close();
    } catch (IOException e) {
        e.printStackTrace();
    }
  }
}
```

2. **Client-Side Code** (Client.java): The client connects to the server and sends a message to the server.

java

```
import java.io.*;
import java.net.*;

public class Client {
    public static void main(String[] args)
{
        try {
            // Create a Socket to connect
to the server on localhost at port 12345
            Socket     socket    =    new
Socket("localhost", 12345);

            // Create output stream to send
data to the server
            PrintWriter   writer   =   new
PrintWriter(socket.getOutputStream(),
true);
```

```
            writer.println("Hello from the
client!");

            // Close the connection
            writer.close();
            socket.close();
        } catch (IOException e) {
            e.printStackTrace();
        }
    }
}
```

Explanation:

- **Server**:
  - The server listens for incoming connections on port 12345.
  - When a client connects, the server reads the message sent by the client and prints it to the console.
- **Client**:
  - The client establishes a connection to the server at localhost on port 12345.
  - The client sends a message to the server using PrintWriter.

Running the Application:

1. First, run the **Server** class.

2. Then, run the **Client** class.

Output on Server Side:

```
arduino
```

```
Server is waiting for a connection...
Client connected.
Received from client: Hello from the client!
```

Working with APIs and Web Services in Java

APIs and web services are a key part of modern software applications, allowing systems to communicate with each other over the internet. In Java, you can use **HTTP** to interact with RESTful APIs or SOAP-based web services.

1. **Using** **HttpURLConnection**: The HttpURLConnection class can be used to make HTTP requests, such as GET, POST, PUT, and DELETE requests, to interact with web APIs.

   Example: Sending a GET Request:

   ```java
   java
   ```

   ```java
   import java.io.*;
   ```

```java
import java.net.*;

public class APIExample {
    public static void main(String[] args) {
        try {
            // URL of the API
            URL url = new URL("https://jsonplaceholder.typicode.com/posts");

            // Create a connection to the API
            HttpURLConnection connection = (HttpURLConnection) url.openConnection();

            connection.setRequestMethod("GET");

            // Read the response
            BufferedReader reader = new BufferedReader(new InputStreamReader(connection.getInputStream()));
            String line;
            while ((line = reader.readLine()) != null) {
                System.out.println(line);
            }
```

214

```
                    // Close the reader
                    reader.close();
            } catch (IOException e) {
                    e.printStackTrace();
            }
        }
    }
```

Explanation:

- We create a `URL` object representing the API endpoint.
- We open a connection using `HttpURLConnection` and set the request method to `GET`.
- We read and print the response from the API.

2. **Using `HttpClient` (Java 11 and above)**: The `HttpClient` class introduced in Java 11 provides a more modern and easier way to work with HTTP requests.

Example: Sending a GET Request with `HttpClient`:

```java
import java.net.URI;
import java.net.http.HttpClient;
import java.net.http.HttpRequest;
import java.net.http.HttpResponse;

public class HttpClientExample {
```

```java
    public static void main(String[] args)
{
        try {
            // Create an HttpClient
            HttpClient      client      =
HttpClient.newHttpClient();

            // Create a GET request
            HttpRequest     request     =
HttpRequest.newBuilder()

.uri(URI.create("https://jsonplaceholder.
typicode.com/posts"))
                    .build();

            // Send the request and get the
response
            HttpResponse<String>  response
=               client.send(request,
HttpResponse.BodyHandlers.ofString());

            // Print the response body

System.out.println(response.body());
        } catch (Exception e) {
            e.printStackTrace();
        }
    }
}
```

Explanation:

- We create an `HttpClient` object to send HTTP requests.
- We build a `GET` request using `HttpRequest.newBuilder()`.
- We send the request and get the response using `client.send()`.
- The response is printed to the console.

Real-World Application: Building a Chat Application

A **chat application** is a good example of a real-time, multi-threaded application that uses networking. We can use **sockets** to create a client-server chat system where multiple clients can send messages to each other through a server.

1. **Server-Side Code for Chat Application**: The server listens for incoming client connections and relays messages to all connected clients.

```java

import java.io.*;
import java.net.*;
import java.util.*;

public class ChatServer {
```

217

```java
    private static final int PORT = 12345;
    private     static     Set<PrintWriter>
clientWriters = new HashSet<>();

    public static void main(String[] args)
{
        System.out.println("Chat    server
started...");
        try (ServerSocket serverSocket =
new ServerSocket(PORT)) {
            while (true) {
                new
ClientHandler(serverSocket.accept()).star
t();
            }
        } catch (IOException e) {
            e.printStackTrace();
        }
    }

    private  static  class  ClientHandler
extends Thread {
        private Socket socket;
        private PrintWriter out;
        private BufferedReader in;

        public        ClientHandler(Socket
socket) {
            this.socket = socket;
```

218

```java
        }

        @Override
        public void run() {
            try {
                in            =            new
BufferedReader(new
InputStreamReader(socket.getInputStream()
));
                out           =            new
PrintWriter(socket.getOutputStream(),
true);

                synchronized
(clientWriters) {

clientWriters.add(out);
                }

                String message;
                while       ((message      =
in.readLine()) != null) {

System.out.println("Received:      "      +
message);
                    synchronized
(clientWriters) {
                        for    (PrintWriter
writer : clientWriters) {
```

```
                writer.println(message);
                                        }
                                    }
                                }
                        } catch (IOException e) {
                            e.printStackTrace();
                        } finally {
                            try {
                                socket.close();
                            } catch (IOException e) {
                                e.printStackTrace();
                            }
                        }
                    }
                }
            }
```

2. **Client-Side Code for Chat Application**: Each client connects to the server and sends/receives messages.

```java
import java.io.*;
import java.net.*;

public class ChatClient {
    private    static    final    String
SERVER_ADDRESS = "localhost";
```

220

```java
    private static final int SERVER_PORT =
12345;

    public static void main(String[] args)
{
        try    (Socket    socket    =    new
Socket(SERVER_ADDRESS, SERVER_PORT);
            BufferedReader  reader  `=  new
BufferedReader(new
InputStreamReader(System.in));
            PrintWriter    writer    =    new
PrintWriter(socket.getOutputStream(),
true);
            BufferedReader serverReader =
new                    BufferedReader(new
InputStreamReader(socket.getInputStream()
))) {

            // Read  messages  from  the
server in a separate thread
            new Thread(() -> {
                try {
                    String message;
                    while   ((message   =
serverReader.readLine()) != null) {

System.out.println("Server: " + message);
                    }
                } catch (IOException e) {
```

221

```
                          e.printStackTrace();
            }
        }).start();

        // Send messages to the server
        String userInput;
        while         ((userInput        =
reader.readLine()) != null) {

writer.println(userInput);
            }
        } catch (IOException e) {
            e.printStackTrace();
        }
    }
}
```

Explanation:

- **Chat Server**: The server listens for incoming client connections and creates a new `ClientHandler` thread for each connection. The server relays messages to all connected clients.
- **Chat Client**: The client connects to the server, reads messages from the user, and sends them to the server. It also listens for incoming messages from the server and displays them.

Running the Chat Application:

222

1. Run the **ChatServer** class.

2. Run multiple instances of the **ChatClient** class to simulate different users.

Summary

In this chapter, we covered:

- **Java Networking**: An introduction to networking concepts using **sockets** for client-server communication and **HTTP** for interacting with web services.

- **Creating a Client-Server Application**: We built a simple chat application where multiple clients can send and receive messages through a server.

- **Working with APIs**: We demonstrated how to interact with APIs using **HttpURLConnection** and **HttpClient** in Java.

- **Real-World Example**: We implemented a multi-threaded chat application to showcase the use of sockets and concurrency.

Java networking and multi-threading are powerful features for building scalable, responsive, and real-time applications. By mastering networking, you can create applications that interact with other systems and users seamlessly.

CHAPTER 19

JAVA SECURITY BASICS

Security is a vital aspect of any software application, particularly when dealing with sensitive data like passwords, personal information, and financial transactions. Java provides a range of tools, libraries, and practices to ensure that your applications are secure and can defend against common vulnerabilities. In this chapter, we will discuss the importance of security in Java applications, cover key concepts like **encryption, hashing**, and **secure communication**, and explore Java security libraries and best practices. Finally, we'll implement a **real-world use case**: a **secure login system** using encryption and hashing.

Importance of Security in Java Applications

Security is crucial for preventing unauthorized access, ensuring data confidentiality, and protecting against malicious activities such as hacking, data theft, and man-in-the-middle attacks. Java, being one of the most widely used programming languages, provides strong built-in security features to ensure that applications are resistant to attacks.

Key security concerns in Java applications include:

1. **Authentication**: Verifying the identity of a user or system.

2. **Authorization**: Ensuring that an authenticated user has the right to access certain resources or perform certain actions.

3. **Data Integrity**: Ensuring that the data has not been tampered with or altered during transmission.

4. **Confidentiality**: Ensuring that sensitive data is protected from unauthorized access.

5. **Non-repudiation**: Ensuring that an action or transaction cannot be denied after it has been executed.

Java provides several libraries and practices to mitigate security risks and protect sensitive data, including the Java Cryptography Architecture (JCA), Java Secure Socket Extension (JSSE), and Java Authentication and Authorization Service (JAAS).

Understanding Encryption, Hashing, and Secure Communication

1. **Encryption**: **Encryption** is the process of converting plaintext into ciphertext using a key. It ensures that data remains confidential and can only be read by authorized parties. There are two main types of encryption:
   - **Symmetric encryption**: The same key is used for both encryption and decryption (e.g., AES, DES).

- o **Asymmetric encryption**: Two keys are used: a public key for encryption and a private key for decryption (e.g., RSA).

Example (Encrypting and decrypting text using AES):

java

```
import javax.crypto.Cipher;
import javax.crypto.KeyGenerator;
import javax.crypto.SecretKey;
import javax.crypto.spec.SecretKeySpec;
import java.util.Base64;

public class EncryptionExample {
    public static void main(String[] args)
throws Exception {
        String    plainText    =    "Hello,
world!";

        // Generate a secret key
        KeyGenerator    keyGenerator    =
KeyGenerator.getInstance("AES");
        keyGenerator.init(128);
        SecretKey    secretKey    =
keyGenerator.generateKey();

        // Encrypt the text
```

226

```
        Cipher          cipher          =
Cipher.getInstance("AES");
        cipher.init(Cipher.ENCRYPT_MODE,
secretKey);
        byte[]          encryptedText    =
cipher.doFinal(plainText.getBytes());

        // Convert the encrypted text to
Base64 for display
        String    encryptedTextBase64    =
Base64.getEncoder().encodeToString(encryp
tedText);
        System.out.println("Encrypted
Text: " + encryptedTextBase64);

        // Decrypt the text
        cipher.init(Cipher.DECRYPT_MODE,
secretKey);
        byte[]          decryptedText    =
cipher.doFinal(Base64.getDecoder().decode
(encryptedTextBase64));
        System.out.println("Decrypted
Text: " + new String(decryptedText));
    }
}
```

Explanation:

- o In this example, we use **AES** symmetric
  encryption to encrypt and decrypt a simple string.

227

o The `SecretKey` is used for both encryption and decryption, and the `Cipher` class handles the encryption and decryption processes.

2. **Hashing**: **Hashing** is a process of converting data into a fixed-size value or hash. It is typically used for verifying the integrity of data and for securely storing passwords. Unlike encryption, hashing is a one-way process, meaning that once data is hashed, it cannot be reversed back to its original form.

Example (Hashing a password using SHA-256):

java

```java
import java.security.MessageDigest;

public class HashingExample {
    public static void main(String[] args)
throws Exception {
        String password = "myPassword123";

        // Create a SHA-256 hash of the
password
        MessageDigest        digest        =
MessageDigest.getInstance("SHA-256");
        byte[]         hashedBytes          =
digest.digest(password.getBytes());
```

```
        // Convert the byte array to a
hexadecimal string
        StringBuilder hexString = new
StringBuilder();
        for (byte b : hashedBytes) {

hexString.append(String.format("%02x",
b));
        }

        System.out.println("Hashed
Password: " + hexString.toString());
    }
}
```

Explanation:

- o In this example, we use **SHA-256** (a cryptographic hash function) to hash a password. The hashed value is a fixed-size string.
- o This ensures that passwords are securely stored in their hashed form, which cannot be easily reverse-engineered.

3. **Secure Communication**: Secure communication ensures that data transmitted over a network is encrypted, maintaining confidentiality and preventing eavesdropping. Java provides the **Java Secure Socket Extension (JSSE)** for implementing secure

communication over sockets using protocols like **SSL/TLS**.

Example (Secure communication using HTTPS):

- o Java's `HttpsURLConnection` class allows you to send secure HTTPS requests and handle SSL/TLS certificates for secure communication.

Java Security Libraries and Practices

1. **Java Cryptography Architecture (JCA)**: The **JCA** provides a framework and API for cryptographic operations, such as encryption, decryption, and hashing. It includes various algorithms like AES, RSA, SHA-256, and others.

2. **Java Secure Socket Extension (JSSE)**: **JSSE** provides the API for implementing secure communication via SSL/TLS. It allows you to set up secure sockets and HTTP connections using SSL/TLS protocols.

3. **Java Authentication and Authorization Service (JAAS)**: **JAAS** allows you to manage user authentication and authorization. It provides a way to authenticate users based on usernames, passwords, and other factors.

4. **Secure Password Storage**: Always store passwords securely by:

- o Hashing passwords before storage.
- o Using strong, modern hashing algorithms like **bcrypt** or **PBKDF2**.
- o Adding a **salt** to passwords before hashing to prevent rainbow table attacks.

Real-World Use Case: Secure Login System

Let's implement a **secure login system** that uses **password hashing** and **encryption** to ensure secure authentication. The system will:

- Hash the user's password before storing it in a database.
- Verify the password by comparing the hashed value during login.

1. **User Login System**: The system will include a `User` class for storing the username and password, and a `LoginSystem` class for handling login logic.

2. **User Class** (`User.java`):

java

```java
public class User {
    private String username;
    private String hashedPassword;
```

```java
        public  User(String  username,  String
hashedPassword) {
            this.username = username;
            this.hashedPassword           =
hashedPassword;
    }

    public String getUsername() {
        return username;
    }

    public String getHashedPassword() {
        return hashedPassword;
    }
}
```

3. **LoginSystem Class** (LoginSystem.java):

java

```java
import java.security.MessageDigest;
import
java.security.NoSuchAlgorithmException;

public class LoginSystem {
    private    static    final    String
SECRET_SALT = "random_salt"; // Simple salt
for demonstration
```

232

```java
public static String
hashPassword(String password) throws
NoSuchAlgorithmException {
    String saltedPassword = password +
SECRET_SALT;
    MessageDigest digest =
MessageDigest.getInstance("SHA-256");
    byte[] hashedBytes =
digest.digest(saltedPassword.getBytes());

    StringBuilder hexString = new
StringBuilder();
    for (byte b : hashedBytes) {

hexString.append(String.format("%02x",
b));
    }

    return hexString.toString();
    }

public static boolean
authenticate(User user, String
enteredPassword) throws
NoSuchAlgorithmException {
    String hashedEnteredPassword =
hashPassword(enteredPassword);
```

233

```java
        return
user.getHashedPassword().equals(hashedEnt
eredPassword);
    }

    public static void main(String[] args)
throws NoSuchAlgorithmException {
        // Simulate storing a user
        String        storedPassword        =
"userPassword123";
        String        hashedPassword        =
hashPassword(storedPassword);
        User  user  =  new  User("john_doe",
hashedPassword);

        // Simulate user login
        String        enteredPassword        =
"userPassword123";
        if                (authenticate(user,
enteredPassword)) {
            System.out.println("Login
successful!");
        } else {
            System.out.println("Invalid
username or password.");
        }
    }
}
```

Explanation:

- **Password Hashing**: We use **SHA-256** to hash the password, appending a `salt` to prevent attackers from using precomputed hashes (rainbow tables).
- **Authentication**: During login, the entered password is hashed and compared with the stored hashed password for verification.

Output:

```
nginx

Login successful!
```

Explanation:

- The user's password is hashed and stored securely.
- During login, the entered password is hashed again and compared with the stored hash to ensure authentication.

Summary

In this chapter, we covered:

- **Importance of Security**: Discussed the importance of securing Java applications by ensuring confidentiality, integrity, and authentication.

- **Encryption and Hashing**: Explained the difference between encryption (for confidentiality) and hashing (for secure storage and data integrity).

- **Java Security Libraries**: Introduced key Java libraries for cryptography (JCA), secure communication (JSSE), and user authentication (JAAS).

- **Real-World Use Case**: Implemented a secure login system using **password hashing** and **encryption**, ensuring that user credentials are stored and verified securely.

Security is a critical aspect of any application, and using Java's built-in tools and libraries, you can ensure that your software is resistant to common threats. In the next chapters, we will continue to explore more advanced Java topics to enhance your programming skills.

CHAPTER 20

JAVA FOR WEB DEVELOPMENT

Java is widely used for developing dynamic and robust web applications. With the power of various frameworks and tools, you can build everything from small web apps to large-scale enterprise applications. In this chapter, we will introduce some popular **Java web frameworks** (such as **Spring** and **JavaServer Faces**), explore **Servlets** and **JSP** (JavaServer Pages), and build a simple web application using Java. Finally, we will implement a real-world example of an **e-commerce website backend**.

Introduction to Java Web Frameworks (Spring, JavaServer Faces)

Java provides several frameworks for developing web applications, each offering a different set of features to simplify and streamline web development.

1. **Spring Framework**:
    o   **Spring** is one of the most widely used frameworks for building Java-based web applications. It provides a comprehensive infrastructure for creating enterprise-grade applications.

- o Spring offers modules for various aspects of application development, such as dependency injection (DI), aspect-oriented programming (AOP), and transaction management.
- o The **Spring MVC** module is specifically used for building web applications and follows the Model-View-Controller (MVC) design pattern.
- o **Spring Boot** makes it even easier by providing a set of conventions and auto-configuration options to quickly create and deploy Java-based web applications.

Key Benefits:

- o Simplifies dependency management using **Inversion of Control (IoC)**.
- o Offers built-in tools for transaction management and security.
- o Supports various view technologies, including **JSP, Thymeleaf**, and **FreeMarker**.
- o Highly extensible with a large ecosystem of plugins and modules.

2. **JavaServer Faces (JSF)**:
    - o **JavaServer Faces (JSF)** is a Java web framework that simplifies the development of user interfaces for Java-based web applications.

- o JSF uses a component-based approach to create reusable UI components, such as buttons, input fields, and tables.
- o It integrates with various back-end technologies, like **JPA** (Java Persistence API), to provide a complete solution for web development.
- o **Managed Beans** and **Facelets** are used to handle the back-end logic and UI rendering, respectively.

Key Benefits:

- o Simplifies UI development with reusable components.
- o Integrates well with other Java EE technologies like EJB (Enterprise JavaBeans) and JPA.
- o Built-in support for navigation and state management.

Servlets and JSP (JavaServer Pages)

Java **Servlets** and **JSP** (JavaServer Pages) are the building blocks of Java-based web applications. Both are part of the Java EE (Enterprise Edition) standard and are used to create dynamic web pages.

1. **Servlets**:

- o A **Servlet** is a Java class that extends the `HttpServlet` class and implements the business logic of a web application.
- o Servlets are executed on the server side and can respond to HTTP requests from clients (browsers).
- o They are mainly used to handle requests and generate dynamic content, like processing form submissions or interacting with databases.

Basic Servlet Example:

```java

import java.io.*;
import javax.servlet.*;
import javax.servlet.http.*;


public class HelloWorldServlet extends HttpServlet {
    protected                          void
doGet(HttpServletRequest              request,
HttpServletResponse     response)      throws
ServletException, IOException {

response.setContentType("text/html");
        PrintWriter          out          =
response.getWriter();
```

```
out.println("<html><body><h1>Hello,
World!</h1></body></html>");
    }
}
```

Explanation:

- o The `doGet` method is called when the servlet handles an HTTP GET request.
- o The `response.getWriter()` method is used to send the output to the client's browser.

2. **JavaServer Pages (JSP)**:
   - o **JSP** is a technology that allows for embedding Java code directly into HTML pages. It simplifies the process of generating dynamic web content.
   - o JSP files are compiled into Servlets by the server, so the execution model is similar to Servlets.
   - o JSP allows developers to create HTML templates with embedded Java code to perform tasks like displaying user data, processing forms, and accessing databases.

Basic JSP Example:

```
jsp
```

```
<html>
```

241

```
<body>
    <h1>Welcome        to        My        Web
Application!</h1>
    <p>The    current   time   is:   <%=   new
java.util.Date() %></p>
</body>
</html>
```

Explanation:

- o The `<%= ... %>` syntax is used to embed Java code inside HTML.
- o In this example, the current time is displayed on the page using Java code inside the JSP.

Building a Simple Web Application Using Java

Now that we've covered the basics of web frameworks, Servlets, and JSP, let's build a simple web application using Java. For this example, we'll create a basic **student management system** that allows adding and viewing students.

1. **Project Setup**:
   - o Use **Maven** to set up a project and include dependencies for Servlets, JSP, and a web server (e.g., Apache Tomcat).

- o The `web.xml` file will define the configuration for the servlet and JSP mappings.

2. **Student Servlet**: The `StudentServlet` will handle the creation and display of student records.

java

```java
import java.io.*;
import javax.servlet.*;
import javax.servlet.http.*;
import java.util.*;

public class StudentServlet extends
HttpServlet {
    private List<String> students = new
ArrayList<>();

    protected                           void
doPost(HttpServletRequest           request,
HttpServletResponse      response)      throws
ServletException, IOException {
        String          studentName          =
request.getParameter("name");
        if   (studentName   !=   null   &&
!studentName.isEmpty()) {
            students.add(studentName);
        }

response.sendRedirect("students.jsp");
```

243

```
    }

    protected                              void
doGet(HttpServletRequest                request,
HttpServletResponse      response)      throws
ServletException, IOException {
        request.setAttribute("students",
students);
        RequestDispatcher    dispatcher    =
request.getRequestDispatcher("students.js
p");
        dispatcher.forward(request,
response);
    }
}
```

Explanation:

- o The doPost method handles adding a new student by reading the student's name from the form data and adding it to the students list.
- o The doGet method forwards the list of students to a JSP page for display.

3. **JSP Page (students.jsp)**: The students.jsp page will display the list of students.

```jsp
jsp

<html>
```

```
<body>
    <h2>Student List</h2>
    <ul>
        <c:forEach            var="student"
items="${students}">
            <li>${student}</li>
        </c:forEach>
    </ul>
    <form            action="StudentServlet"
method="POST">
        <label   for="name">Enter   student
name: </label>
        <input    type="text"    id="name"
name="name" required>
        <button            type="submit">Add
Student</button>
    </form>
</body>
</html>
```

Explanation:

- The c:forEach tag is used to iterate over the list of students and display each student's name.
- The form allows the user to input a student's name, which is sent to the StudentServlet for processing.

4. **web.xml Configuration**: The web.xml file configures the servlet and JSP mappings.

245

xml

```
<web-app
xmlns="http://java.sun.com/xml/ns/javaee"
xmlns:xsi="http://www.w3.org/2001/XMLSche
ma-instance"

xsi:schemaLocation="http://java.sun.com/x
ml/ns/javaee
http://java.sun.com/xml/ns/javaee/web-
app_3_0.xsd"
    version="3.0">
    <servlet>
        <servlet-
name>StudentServlet</servlet-name>
        <servlet-
class>StudentServlet</servlet-class>
    </servlet>
    <servlet-mapping>
        <servlet-
name>StudentServlet</servlet-name>
        <url-
pattern>/StudentServlet</url-pattern>
    </servlet-mapping>
</web-app>
```

Explanation:

o The `web.xml` file defines the `StudentServlet` and maps it to the URL pattern `/StudentServlet`.

Real-World Example: E-Commerce Website Backend

In a real-world application, an **e-commerce website** backend typically involves managing products, users, orders, and payments. For simplicity, let's consider the **product management** part of the system.

1. **Product Model**: We define a `Product` class with properties like `id`, `name`, `price`, and `description`.
2. **ProductServlet**: The servlet handles the CRUD operations for products, such as adding, viewing, and deleting products.
3. **Product Database**: You would typically use a database (e.g., MySQL) to store product data, but for simplicity, we'll store products in memory in a `List` or `Map`.
4. **ProductPage (JSP)**: The JSP page allows administrators to view and manage products.

Summary

In this chapter, we covered the basics of **Java web development**:

- **Java Web Frameworks**: We discussed popular frameworks like **Spring** and **JavaServer Faces (JSF)** for building Java-based web applications.
- **Servlets and JSP**: We explained how to use Servlets and JSP to create dynamic web content, manage HTTP requests, and generate dynamic HTML pages.
- **Building a Simple Web Application**: We built a basic **student management system** using Servlets and JSP.
- **Real-World Use Case**: We demonstrated how to create a basic **e-commerce backend** for managing products.

Java offers powerful tools for web development, allowing you to build dynamic, scalable, and secure applications. With frameworks like Spring, you can rapidly develop complex enterprise applications, while Servlets and JSP provide a lower-level approach to web development for fine-grained control. In the next chapters, we will continue to explore more advanced topics in Java.

CHAPTER 21

INTRODUCTION TO DESIGN PATTERNS IN JAVA

Design patterns are reusable solutions to common problems in software design. They provide best practices for writing flexible, scalable, and maintainable code. In Java, design patterns play a crucial role in structuring code that can be easily understood and modified, especially in complex applications. In this chapter, we will introduce design patterns, explain why they matter, and explore some common design patterns in Java, including **Singleton**, **Factory**, and **Observer**. We will also implement these patterns with real-world examples and discuss a case study of using the **Singleton pattern** for configuration management.

What Are Design Patterns and Why They Matter?

Design patterns are general solutions to recurring design problems in software development. They are not ready-to-use code but rather guidelines or templates that you can adapt to solve specific problems in your application.

Why do design patterns matter?

1. **Code Reusability**: Design patterns encourage the reuse of successful solutions, saving time and effort.

2. **Maintainability**: A well-structured design makes it easier to maintain and modify the code in the future.

3. **Scalability**: Many design patterns are built with scalability in mind, allowing the system to grow without major refactoring.

4. **Communication**: Design patterns provide a shared vocabulary for developers, making it easier to communicate complex design decisions.

By following proven design patterns, developers can create more flexible and robust systems. Let's explore a few of the most common design patterns used in Java.

Common Design Patterns in Java

1. **Singleton Pattern**: The **Singleton pattern** ensures that a class has only one instance and provides a global point of access to that instance. This is useful when you need to control access to shared resources, like a configuration file or a database connection pool.

   Example: A **Configuration Manager** that ensures only one instance of the configuration settings is used throughout the application.

Implementation of Singleton:

java

```java
public class ConfigurationManager {
    private static ConfigurationManager
instance;

    // Private constructor to prevent
instantiation
    private ConfigurationManager() {
        // Initialize configuration
settings
    }

    // Public method to provide access to
the instance
    public static synchronized
ConfigurationManager getInstance() {
        if (instance == null) {
            instance = new
ConfigurationManager();
        }
        return instance;
    }

    public void printConfiguration() {
        System.out.println("Configuration
Settings: [Sample Configuration]");
    }
```

```
}
```

Explanation:

- o **Private Constructor**: The constructor is private, ensuring that new instances cannot be created outside the class.
- o **Static Method**: The `getInstance()` method is static and synchronized to ensure that only one instance of the class is created.

Using the Singleton:

```
java
```

```java
public class Main {
    public static void main(String[] args)
{
        ConfigurationManager    config    =
ConfigurationManager.getInstance();
        config.printConfiguration();
    }
}
```

Output:

```
pgsql
```

```
Configuration         Settings:       [Sample
Configuration]
```

2. **Factory Pattern**: The **Factory pattern** provides a way to create objects without specifying the exact class of object that will be created. It defines an interface for creating objects, but the implementation is left to the subclasses.

   Example: Creating different types of vehicles (Car, Bike) without specifying the exact class type at the time of object creation.

   Implementation of Factory:

```java
interface Vehicle {
    void drive();
}

class Car implements Vehicle {
    @Override
    public void drive() {
        System.out.println("Driving       a
car...");
    }
}

class Bike implements Vehicle {
```

253

```java
    @Override
    public void drive() {
        System.out.println("Riding        a
bike...");
    }
}


class VehicleFactory {
    public          static          Vehicle
getVehicle(String type) {
        if   ("Car".equalsIgnoreCase(type))
{
            return new Car();
        }              else              if
("Bike".equalsIgnoreCase(type)) {
            return new Bike();
        } else {
            throw                        new
IllegalArgumentException("Invalid   vehicle
type");
        }
    }
}
```

Using the Factory:

```java
java


public class Main {
```

```
    public static void main(String[] args)
{

        Vehicle        vehicle1        =
VehicleFactory.getVehicle("Car");
        vehicle1.drive();


        Vehicle        vehicle2        =
VehicleFactory.getVehicle("Bike");
        vehicle2.drive();
    }
}
```

Output:

css

Driving a car...
Riding a bike...

Explanation:

o The VehicleFactory class decides which
concrete Vehicle object to create based on the
input. This decouples the client code from the
specific classes of objects it uses.

3. **Observer Pattern**: The **Observer pattern** defines a one-
to-many dependency between objects so that when one
object changes state, all its dependents (observers) are

255

notified and updated automatically. This pattern is commonly used in implementing event handling systems.

Example: A stock price monitoring system, where multiple users (observers) are notified whenever the stock price (subject) changes.

Implementation of Observer:

java

```java
import java.util.ArrayList;
import java.util.List;

interface Observer {
    void update(String stockPrice);
}

class StockPrice implements Subject {
    private List<Observer> observers = new
ArrayList<>();
    private String stockPrice;

    @Override
    public    void    addObserver(Observer
observer) {
        observers.add(observer);
    }
```

```java
    @Override
    public   void   removeObserver(Observer
observer) {
        observers.remove(observer);
    }


    @Override
    public void notifyObservers() {
        for     (Observer     observer     :
observers) {
            observer.update(stockPrice);
        }
    }


    public    void    setStockPrice(String
stockPrice) {
        this.stockPrice = stockPrice;
        notifyObservers();
    }
}

class    StockPriceObserver    implements
Observer {
    private String observerName;

    public       StockPriceObserver(String
observerName) {
        this.observerName = observerName;
    }
```

257

```java
    @Override
    public void update(String stockPrice)
{
        System.out.println(observerName +
" received stock price update: " +
stockPrice);
    }
}
```

Using the Observer Pattern:

java

```java
public class Main {
    public static void main(String[] args)
{
        StockPrice stockPrice = new
StockPrice();
        StockPriceObserver observer1 = new
StockPriceObserver("Observer 1");
        StockPriceObserver observer2 = new
StockPriceObserver("Observer 2");


stockPrice.addObserver(observer1);


stockPrice.addObserver(observer2);
```

```
stockPrice.setStockPrice("$100.50");

stockPrice.setStockPrice("$101.75");
    }
}
```

Output:

```
pgsql

Observer 1 received stock price update:
$100.50
Observer 2 received stock price update:
$100.50
Observer 1 received stock price update:
$101.75
Observer 2 received stock price update:
$101.75
```

Explanation:

o   The StockPrice class is the **subject**, and the StockPriceObserver class is the **observer**. When the stock price changes, all observers are notified and updated automatically.

In many enterprise applications, configuration settings such as database URLs, API keys, or file paths need to be shared across different parts of the application. The **Singleton pattern** is perfect for managing such global settings because it ensures that only one instance of the configuration object exists.

1. **Configuration Manager**: We can use the Singleton pattern to implement a **ConfigurationManager** class, which loads the application's configuration from a file and provides global access to these settings.

java

```java
public class ConfigurationManager {
    private static ConfigurationManager instance;
    private String databaseUrl;
    private String apiKey;

    private ConfigurationManager() {
        // Load configuration settings
from a file or database
        this.databaseUrl =
"jdbc:mysql://localhost:3306/mydb";
        this.apiKey = "API-KEY-12345";
    }
```

```java
    public        static        synchronized
ConfigurationManager getInstance() {
        if (instance == null) {
            instance        =        new
ConfigurationManager();
        }
        return instance;
    }

    public String getDatabaseUrl() {
        return databaseUrl;
    }

    public String getApiKey() {
        return apiKey;
    }
}
```

Using the ConfigurationManager:

java

```java
public class Main {
    public static void main(String[] args)
{
        ConfigurationManager config    =
ConfigurationManager.getInstance();
        System.out.println("Database    URL:
" + config.getDatabaseUrl());
```

261

```
        System.out.println("API  Key:  "  +
config.getApiKey());
    }
}
```

Output:

```
bash

Database                              URL:
jdbc:mysql://localhost:3306/mydb
API Key: API-KEY-12345
```

Explanation:

- The **ConfigurationManager** is implemented as a Singleton, ensuring that only one instance is used throughout the application.
- It holds global configuration values, such as `databaseUrl` and `apiKey`, and provides access to these values via getter methods.

Summary

In this chapter, we:

- **Introduced Design Patterns**: Explained what design patterns are and why they are important for writing maintainable and scalable software.
- **Covered Common Design Patterns**:
  - **Singleton**: Ensures that a class has only one instance and provides a global point of access.
  - **Factory**: Allows you to create objects without specifying the exact class of object to be created.
  - **Observer**: Defines a one-to-many dependency, allowing objects to be notified when the state of another object changes.
- **Implemented Real-World Examples**: We used the **Singleton pattern** to manage application configuration settings in a secure and efficient way.

Design patterns are essential for building well-structured and maintainable Java applications. By mastering these patterns, you can solve common design problems and improve the overall architecture of your software. In the next chapters, we will continue to explore more advanced Java concepts and their practical applications.

CHAPTER 22

UNIT TESTING IN JAVA

Unit testing is a fundamental part of writing reliable and maintainable Java applications. It involves testing individual units of code, such as methods or classes, to ensure that they behave as expected. **JUnit** is the most widely used framework for unit testing in Java, allowing developers to automate the testing process and identify bugs early in the development cycle. In this chapter, we will introduce unit testing with **JUnit**, explain how to write and run test cases, explore **mocking** and **Test-Driven Development (TDD)**, and demonstrate unit testing with a **real-world example**: testing a simple calculator class.

Introduction to Unit Testing with JUnit

JUnit is a widely-used testing framework for Java that provides annotations and assertions to write and run tests for Java code. It helps automate testing and ensures that code behaves as expected, making it an essential tool for developers.

1. **JUnit Annotations**:

   o `@Test`: Marks a method as a test case.

- o `@Before`: Executes before each test method. Used for setting up common test fixtures.

- o `@After`: Executes after each test method. Used for cleaning up after tests.

- o `@BeforeClass`: Executes once before any test methods in the class. Typically used for expensive setup operations.

- o `@AfterClass`: Executes once after all test methods in the class.

2. **JUnit Assertions**: Assertions are methods used to check if the expected outcome matches the actual result. Common assertions include:

- o `assertEquals(expected, actual)`: Checks if two values are equal.

- o `assertNotNull(object)`: Checks if an object is not null.

- o `assertTrue(condition)`: Checks if the condition is true.

- o `assertFalse(condition)`: Checks if the condition is false.

Writing and Running Test Cases

1. **Setting up JUnit in your Project**: If you're using Maven, you can include the JUnit dependency in your `pom.xml`:

xml

```xml
<dependency>
    <groupId>junit</groupId>
    <artifactId>junit</artifactId>
    <version>4.13.2</version>
    <scope>test</scope>
</dependency>
```

For Gradle, add this dependency:

gradle

```gradle
testImplementation 'junit:junit:4.13.2'
```

2. **Writing a Simple Test Case**: In JUnit, a test case is a method that verifies a piece of functionality. Here's an example of a simple test case that checks if the addition operation of a calculator is correct:

Calculator Class:

java

```java
public class Calculator {
    public int add(int a, int b) {
        return a + b;
    }

    public int subtract(int a, int b) {
```

266

```
        return a - b;
    }
}
```

Test Case for Calculator:

```java
import org.junit.Test;
import static org.junit.Assert.*;

public class CalculatorTest {

    @Test
    public void testAdd() {
        Calculator    calculator    =    new
Calculator();
        int result = calculator.add(2, 3);
        assertEquals(5,    result);       //
Verifying that 2 + 3 = 5
    }

    @Test
    public void testSubtract() {
        Calculator    calculator    =    new
Calculator();
        int           result            =
calculator.subtract(5, 3);
        assertEquals(2,    result);       //
Verifying that 5 - 3 = 2
```

```
    }
}
```

Explanation:

- o We created a `Calculator` class with `add` and `subtract` methods.

- o We wrote JUnit test methods `testAdd` and `testSubtract` to verify the correctness of these methods.

- o The `assertEquals` method compares the expected result with the actual result.

3. **Running the Test Cases**:

- o In **Eclipse** or **IntelliJ**, right-click the test class or method and select "Run" to execute the test.

- o In **Maven**, use the command `mvn test` to run tests.

- o In **Gradle**, use the command `gradle test` to execute the tests.

Mocking and Test-Driven Development (TDD)

1. **Mocking**: **Mocking** is the practice of creating mock objects that simulate the behavior of real objects in the system. It is useful when testing components that depend

on external systems (like databases or APIs), as it allows you to isolate the unit being tested.

- o Popular mocking libraries in Java: **Mockito** and **EasyMock**.

Example of mocking with **Mockito**:

```java
import static org.mockito.Mockito.*;

public class ServiceTest {

    @Test
    public void testServiceMethod() {
        // Create a mock object for the
dependent class
        Database        mockDatabase    =
mock(Database.class);

when(mockDatabase.getData()).thenReturn("
Mocked Data");

        // Use the mock object in the
service
        Service     service     =     new
Service(mockDatabase);
        String          result          =
service.fetchData();
```

```
        assertEquals("Mocked        Data",
result);  // Assert the mocked response
    }
}
```

Explanation:

- o We created a mock object for the `Database` class using Mockito's `mock()` method.
- o We used the `when()` and `thenReturn()` methods to define the behavior of the mock object.
- o The `Service` class uses the mocked `Database` object to fetch data, and we verify that the mocked data is returned.

2. **Test-Driven Development (TDD)**: **TDD** is a development approach where you write tests before writing the actual code. The basic cycle in TDD is:

    1. **Write a test**: Write a test case for the functionality you want to implement.
    2. **Run the test**: Run the test, which should fail initially because the functionality is not implemented yet.
    3. **Write the code**: Implement the code to make the test pass.

4. **Refactor**: Refactor the code while keeping the test passing.

Example of TDD Cycle:

o **Step 1**: Write a test case for a method that calculates the area of a circle.

o **Step 2**: Run the test (it should fail).

o **Step 3**: Implement the `calculateArea` method to pass the test.

o **Step 4**: Refactor the method if necessary while keeping the test passing.

Real-World Example: Testing a Calculator Class

In a real-world scenario, you might need to test a more complex `Calculator` class that supports multiple operations like addition, subtraction, multiplication, and division. Let's extend our `Calculator` class and write unit tests for each method.

1. **Calculator Class** (Extended):

```java
public class Calculator {

    public int add(int a, int b) {
```

```java
        return a + b;
    }

    public int subtract(int a, int b) {
        return a - b;
    }

    public int multiply(int a, int b) {
        return a * b;
    }

    public double divide(int a, int b) {
        if (b == 0) {
            throw                    new
IllegalArgumentException("Cannot divide by
zero");
        }
        return (double) a / b;
    }
}
```

2. Test Class:

```java
java

import org.junit.Test;
import static org.junit.Assert.*;

public class CalculatorTest {
```

```java
    private final Calculator calculator =
new Calculator();

    @Test
    public void testAdd() {
        assertEquals(5,  calculator.add(2,
3));
    }

    @Test
    public void testSubtract() {
        assertEquals(2,
calculator.subtract(5, 3));
    }

    @Test
    public void testMultiply() {
        assertEquals(6,
calculator.multiply(2, 3));
    }

    @Test
    public void testDivide() {
        assertEquals(2.0,
calculator.divide(6, 3), 0.0);
    }

    @Test(expected                        =
IllegalArgumentException.class)
```

273

```
public void testDivideByZero() {
    calculator.divide(1,    0);        //
Should throw IllegalArgumentException
    }
}
```

Explanation:

- o We extended the `Calculator` class with `multiply` and `divide` methods.
- o The `CalculatorTest` class tests all the operations.
- o The `testDivideByZero` method checks that dividing by zero throws an exception.

3. **Running the Tests**: Run the tests using your IDE, Maven, or Gradle to ensure that all tests pass. If any test fails, fix the code and rerun the tests.

Summary

In this chapter, we covered the following key concepts in **unit testing** with JUnit:

- **JUnit Basics**: We introduced JUnit and demonstrated how to write and run unit tests using annotations and assertions.

- **Mocking**: We discussed how to use mocking (with libraries like Mockito) to simulate external dependencies in tests.

- **Test-Driven Development (TDD)**: We introduced TDD as a methodology for writing tests before writing code, improving software quality and maintainability.

- **Real-World Example**: We extended our calculator class and wrote unit tests to ensure that it works correctly for all operations, including handling exceptions.

Unit testing is an essential part of modern software development. By writing tests for your code, you can ensure that it behaves as expected, handle edge cases, and improve the quality of your applications. In the next chapters, we will continue to explore more advanced Java techniques and best practices.

CHAPTER 23

JAVA REFLECTION API

The **Java Reflection API** is a powerful tool that allows you to inspect and manipulate classes, methods, fields, and other members of Java programs at runtime. Reflection provides a way for programs to introspect themselves, dynamically load classes, and invoke methods or modify fields without knowing the exact class type at compile time. While reflection can provide flexibility and power, it also comes with performance overhead and security concerns. In this chapter, we will explore **reflection**, how it works, how to use it to inspect and modify classes at runtime, and discuss a **real-world use case** for dynamically creating instances of classes.

What Is Reflection and How Does It Work?

Reflection allows you to examine or modify the behavior of classes, methods, fields, and constructors at runtime. It is a part of the **java.lang.reflect** package and provides several useful classes and methods, such as `Class`, `Method`, `Field`, and `Constructor`. Reflection is commonly used in frameworks like Spring and Hibernate, which need to operate dynamically on objects and classes.

Key Features of Reflection:

1. **Access to Class Metadata**: You can access information about a class, such as its name, methods, fields, and annotations, at runtime.

2. **Dynamic Method Invocation**: You can invoke methods dynamically without knowing the method at compile time.

3. **Modifying Fields**: Reflection allows you to read and write values to fields, even if they are private.

4. **Creating Objects Dynamically**: You can instantiate classes dynamically using the `newInstance()` method.

Using Reflection to Inspect and Modify Classes at Runtime

1. **Getting Class Information**: The `Class` class is at the core of Java reflection. You can obtain the `Class` object of a class using several methods:

   o `Class.forName(String className)` — Loads a class by name.

   o `Object.getClass()` — Gets the `Class` object of an instance.

   o `ClassName.class` — A shorthand to get the `Class` object.

Example:

```java

public class Example {
    public static void main(String[] args)
{
        // Using Class.forName() to get the
Class object
        try {
            Class<?>        clazz        =
Class.forName("java.lang.String");
            System.out.println("Class
name: " + clazz.getName());

            // Get the methods of the class

System.out.println("Methods:");
            for (java.lang.reflect.Method
method : clazz.getDeclaredMethods()) {

System.out.println(method.getName());
            }
        } catch (ClassNotFoundException e)
{
            e.printStackTrace();
        }
    }
}
```

Explanation:

- The `Class.forName()` method loads the `String` class dynamically.
- We use `getDeclaredMethods()` to retrieve all the methods of the `String` class.

2. **Inspecting Fields**: Reflection allows you to inspect the fields (both public and private) of a class and modify them at runtime. The `Field` class provides methods for accessing and changing field values.

Example:

java

```java
import java.lang.reflect.Field;

public class Person {
    private String name;
    private int age;

    public Person(String name, int age) {
        this.name = name;
        this.age = age;
    }

    public String getName() {
        return name;
    }

    public int getAge() {
```

279

```java
        return age;
    }
}


public class ReflectionExample {
    public static void main(String[] args)
{
        try {
            // Create a Person object
            Person     person     =     new
Person("John", 30);

            // Get the 'name' field of the
Person class
            Field     nameField     =
Person.class.getDeclaredField("name");

nameField.setAccessible(true);    // Allow
access to private field

            // Modify the 'name' field of
the person object
            nameField.set(person, "Jane");

            // Output the modified name
            System.out.println("Modified
Name: " + person.getName());
        } catch (NoSuchFieldException |
IllegalAccessException e) {
```

```
            e.printStackTrace();
        }
    }
}
```

Explanation:

- We used `getDeclaredField("name")` to access the private `name` field of the `Person` class.
- `setAccessible(true)` allows access to private fields.
- The `set()` method modifies the field's value.

3. **Invoking Methods Dynamically**: Reflection also enables you to invoke methods on objects dynamically without knowing the method at compile time.

Example:

```java
import java.lang.reflect.Method;

public class Greeting {
    public void greet(String name) {
        System.out.println("Hello, " +
name);
    }
}
```

```java
public class MethodInvocationExample {
    public static void main(String[] args)
{
        try {
            // Create an instance of
Greeting class
            Greeting greeting = new
Greeting();

            // Get the greet method
            Method method =
Greeting.class.getMethod("greet",
String.class);

            // Invoke the greet method
dynamically
            method.invoke(greeting,
"Alice");
        } catch (Exception e) {
            e.printStackTrace();
        }
    }
}
```

Explanation:

o   We used `getMethod()` to obtain a reference to the `greet` method of the `Greeting` class.

- o The `invoke()` method is used to call the method on the `greeting` object with the parameter `"Alice"`.

Real-World Use Case: Dynamically Creating Instances of Classes

In many scenarios, such as plugin-based systems or dependency injection, you may need to create instances of classes dynamically at runtime. The Reflection API allows you to instantiate classes without knowing the exact class type at compile time.

Example: Dynamic Object Creation:

Let's say we want to dynamically create instances of different shapes (e.g., `Circle`, `Square`, `Rectangle`) based on user input. Using reflection, we can instantiate these shapes without explicitly mentioning the class names.

1. **Shape Classes**:

```java
public interface Shape {
    void draw();
}

public class Circle implements Shape {
```

283

```java
    @Override
    public void draw() {
        System.out.println("Drawing      a
Circle");
    }
}


public class Square implements Shape {
    @Override
    public void draw() {
        System.out.println("Drawing      a
Square");
    }
}


public class Rectangle implements Shape {
    @Override
    public void draw() {
        System.out.println("Drawing      a
Rectangle");
    }
}
```

2. **ShapeFactory (Using Reflection to Create Instances)**:

```java
java

import java.lang.reflect.Constructor;

public class ShapeFactory {
```

```java
    public static Shape createShape(String
shapeType) throws Exception {
        // Build the class name dynamically
(Shape + shapeType)
        String className = "com.example."
+ shapeType;
        Class<?>        shapeClass        =
Class.forName(className);
        Constructor<?>    constructor    =
shapeClass.getConstructor();
        return                    (Shape)
constructor.newInstance();    // Create an
instance dynamically
    }
}
```

3. **Main Application**:

```java
java

public class Main {
    public static void main(String[] args)
{
        try {
            Shape        shape        =
ShapeFactory.createShape("Circle");    //
Dynamically create a Circle
            shape.draw();    // Output:
Drawing a Circle
```

285

```
            shape              =
ShapeFactory.createShape("Square");      //
Dynamically create a Square
            shape.draw();      //  Output:
Drawing a Square
        } catch (Exception e) {
            e.printStackTrace();
        }
    }
}
```

Explanation:

- o The `ShapeFactory.createShape()` method builds the class name dynamically by concatenating `"com.example."` (package name) with the shape type (`Circle`, `Square`, etc.).

- o The class is loaded using `Class.forName()`, and its constructor is invoked using reflection to create an instance of the appropriate shape.

Output:

css

```
Drawing a Circle
Drawing a Square
```

286

Summary

In this chapter, we:

- **Introduced Reflection**: We explored how reflection allows you to inspect and modify classes, methods, fields, and constructors at runtime.

- **Inspected and Modified Classes at Runtime**: We used the `Class` class to inspect classes, and `Method`, `Field`, and `Constructor` classes to invoke methods and access fields dynamically.

- **Implemented a Real-World Use Case**: We used reflection to dynamically create instances of different classes, such as shapes, based on user input, demonstrating the flexibility of reflection in real-world applications.

Reflection is a powerful feature in Java that allows you to write flexible and reusable code, but it should be used judiciously due to performance and security concerns. In the next chapters, we will continue to explore advanced Java concepts and techniques for building robust applications.

CHAPTER 24

JAVA ANNOTATIONS

Annotations are a powerful feature in Java that allows developers to attach metadata to Java code. This metadata can be used by compilers, development tools, frameworks, and runtime environments to provide additional behavior or validation during the execution of a program. Annotations are commonly used in frameworks like Spring, Hibernate, and JUnit to automate tasks such as dependency injection, database mapping, and unit testing. In this chapter, we will discuss what annotations are, why they are useful, and how to use both built-in and custom annotations in Java. We will also explore a real-world use case for creating and using custom annotations for **logging**.

What Are Annotations and Why Are They Useful?

Annotations are a way to provide additional information about code without changing the code itself. They are metadata that can be applied to classes, methods, fields, parameters, and other code elements. Annotations do not affect the execution of the program directly, but they can be processed by various tools, compilers, or frameworks to influence behavior, provide validation, or generate code.

Why are annotations useful?

1. **Code Clarity and Readability**: Annotations help make the code more declarative, making it easier to understand the behavior of the code.

2. **Automation**: They enable frameworks and libraries to perform automatic processing based on annotations, reducing boilerplate code.

3. **Validation**: Some annotations provide ways to validate code at compile-time or runtime (e.g., `@NotNull`, `@Size`).

4. **Tooling**: Annotations are widely used in code analysis tools, such as IDEs, build systems, and testing frameworks, to facilitate various operations like unit testing or code generation.

Common Java Annotations

Java provides several built-in annotations, each serving a specific purpose. Here are some of the most commonly used annotations:

1. **@Override**:
   - The `@Override` annotation is used to indicate that a method is overriding a method from its superclass.

- o It helps the compiler identify errors if the method signature does not match the method in the superclass.

Example:

java

```
public class Animal {
    public void makeSound() {
        System.out.println("Animal makes a
sound");
    }
}


public class Dog extends Animal {
    @Override
    public void makeSound() {
        System.out.println("Dog barks");
    }
}
```

Explanation:

- o The @Override annotation helps ensure that the makeSound method in the Dog class is correctly overriding the method in the Animal class. If there is a mistake in the method signature, the compiler will produce an error.

2. **@Deprecated**:

   o The `@Deprecated` annotation marks methods, classes, or fields that are no longer recommended for use. It informs other developers that the annotated code is outdated and may be removed in the future.

Example:

```java
public class OldClass {
    @Deprecated
    public void oldMethod() {
        System.out.println("This is an old method");
    }
}
```

Explanation:

   o The `oldMethod` is marked as deprecated, meaning it should no longer be used. It serves as a warning to developers that they should look for an alternative.

3. **@SuppressWarnings**:

   o The `@SuppressWarnings` annotation is used to suppress specific compiler warnings, such as unchecked type warnings or deprecation warnings.

Example:

```java
@SuppressWarnings("deprecation")
public class Test {
    public void useDeprecatedMethod() {
        OldClass old = new OldClass();
        old.oldMethod(); // This will not show a deprecation warning due to the annotation
    }
}
```

Explanation:

- The `@SuppressWarnings("deprecation")` annotation prevents the compiler from showing warnings about deprecated methods.

4. **@FunctionalInterface**:
   - The `@FunctionalInterface` annotation is used to declare a functional interface, which is an interface with a single abstract method (used primarily for lambda expressions and method references).

292

Example:

```java
java

@FunctionalInterface
public interface MyFunctionalInterface {
    void myMethod();
}
```

Explanation:

- o The `@FunctionalInterface` annotation ensures that the interface contains exactly one abstract method. If it contains more than one, the compiler will throw an error.

Custom Java Annotations

In addition to built-in annotations, Java allows developers to create their own custom annotations. Custom annotations are useful when you need to add specific behavior or metadata to your code that is not covered by built-in annotations.

Creating a Custom Annotation: To create a custom annotation, you use the `@interface` keyword.

1. **Defining a Custom Annotation**:

```
java

import java.lang.annotation.ElementType;
import java.lang.annotation.Retention;
import
java.lang.annotation.RetentionPolicy;
import java.lang.annotation.Target;

@Retention(RetentionPolicy.RUNTIME)      //
Retain at runtime
@Target(ElementType.METHOD)  // Applicable
to methods only
public @interface LogExecution {
    String   value()   default   "Executing
method";
}
```

Explanation:

- o @Retention(RetentionPolicy.RUNTIME):
  This ensures that the annotation is available at
  runtime for reflection.
- o @Target(ElementType.METHOD): This
  restricts the annotation to be used only on
  methods.

2. **Using the Custom Annotation**:

```
java
```

```java
public class Calculator {
    @LogExecution("Adding numbers")
    public int add(int a, int b) {
        return a + b;
    }

    @LogExecution("Subtracting numbers")
    public int subtract(int a, int b) {
        return a - b;
    }
}
```

Explanation:

○ The @LogExecution annotation is applied to methods add and subtract with a custom message.

3. **Processing the Custom Annotation**: You can use **reflection** to process custom annotations at runtime.

Example: Log execution of methods annotated with @LogExecution.

```java
java

import java.lang.annotation.Annotation;
import java.lang.reflect.Method;

public class AnnotationProcessor {
```

```
    public static void main(String[] args)
throws Exception {
        Calculator    calculator    =    new
Calculator();

        // Process methods annotated with
@LogExecution
        for       (Method       method       :
Calculator.class.getDeclaredMethods()) {
            if
(method.isAnnotationPresent(LogExecution.
class)) {
                LogExecution   logExecution
=
method.getAnnotation(LogExecution.class);

System.out.println(logExecution.value()   +
": " + method.getName());
                method.invoke(calculator,
5, 3);   // Dynamically invoke the method
            }
        }
    }
}
```

Explanation:

o We use reflection to inspect the `Calculator` class for methods annotated with `@LogExecution`.

o For each method that has the `@LogExecution` annotation, we retrieve the annotation and print the log message before invoking the method.

Output:

```yaml
Adding numbers: add
Subtracting numbers: subtract
```

Explanation:

o The annotation processor dynamically invokes the methods and logs the execution as per the `@LogExecution` annotation.

Real-World Use Case: Creating and Using Custom Annotations for Logging

Custom annotations are extremely useful for adding behavior to code, especially for tasks like logging. In this case, we've created a custom annotation (`@LogExecution`) to log the execution of methods in the `Calculator` class.

297

This concept can be extended to logging in more complex applications. For example:

- You can create annotations for logging method entry and exit.
- Annotations can be used for tracking performance (e.g., logging the time taken by a method).
- Annotations can be used for tracing method calls in debugging or error handling.

Advanced Use Case: In large-scale systems, annotations like `@Transactional` in Spring help manage transactions, or `@Cacheable` helps manage caching. By using custom annotations, developers can avoid writing repetitive code for logging, caching, and transaction management, improving both code maintainability and clarity.

Summary

In this chapter, we covered:

- **Java Annotations**: An introduction to what annotations are, why they are useful, and how they enhance Java code by adding metadata and automation.
- **Common Java Annotations**: We explored common built-in annotations like `@Override`, `@Deprecated`, and

`@FunctionalInterface`, which serve specific purposes.

- **Custom Java Annotations**: We created and used a custom annotation `@LogExecution` to log method execution dynamically using Java Reflection.
- **Real-World Example**: We demonstrated how to use custom annotations in a practical logging scenario, which is an essential feature for large-scale enterprise applications.

Annotations are a powerful tool in Java, helping developers write clean, maintainable, and reusable code. They are widely used in Java frameworks to simplify tasks like logging, caching, and transaction management. In the next chapters, we will continue exploring more advanced Java topics.